"If someone says he can't do it, don't listen! Tell him to have confidence."
—Antonio (scientist)

"If we knew what it was we were doing, it would not be called research, would it?"
—Albert Einstein

"If you can't change it, work with it."
—Nicole (scientist)

TRY THIS!

EXTREME

50 FUN & SAFE EXPERIMENTS FOR THE MAD SCIENTIST IN YOU

KAREN ROMANO YOUNG
Photographs by **MATTHEW RAKOLA**

NATIONAL
GEOGRAPHIC

WASHINGTON, D.C.

CONTENTS

SAFETY TIPS & GUIDELINES

DEAR PARENTS:

The experiments in this book have been designed to engage your child in fun, creative, and challenging ways. Although we recommend that your young scientist have adult supervision for ALL of the activities and experiments in this book, certain experiments REQUIRE adult supervision. These experiments SHOULD NOT be conducted UNLESS an ADULT is actively involved in the experiment. The ADULT should also perform the riskier parts of the experiment. We have flagged these experiments with "Supervision" labels at the beginning of each experiment for which it is required.

Before you begin an experiment, please read and discuss the following SAFETY GUIDELINES with the child or children involved BEFORE they perform any of the experiments in this book. This will ensure that the guidelines are followed as your young scientist works through the various projects.

SAFETY GUIDELINES

1 **We know you know this, but it's worth repeating. Use extra caution** when working with dry ice, matches, flames, chemicals, sharp knives or scissors, or hot objects.

2 **Prepare yourself** to work in a safe manner (e.g., use safety goggles when working with chemicals or projectiles, chemical safety gloves when working with chemicals, heat-resistant mitts when working with hot objects, no loose clothes or loose hair while working with flames).

3 **Create a safe work space** (e.g., no paper or other combustible items nearby when working with heat or flames, no food or beverages in your work area, if you're using chemicals choose an area with appropriate ventilation, choose an area that younger siblings or the family pet cannot enter unexpectedly).

4 **Have safety equipment on hand** (e.g., have a fire extinguisher, baking soda, or other fire response tools nearby when working with flames; have a first aid kit in the house).

5 **Wash and dry your hands** before and after each experiment.

6 **Follow the directions** for each experiment, and TAKE YOUR TIME.

7 **Read and follow the safety tips** in this book, the guidelines on all product labels, and use your own common sense and judgment.

TIPS FOR...

CHEMICALS such as bleach or other irritants:
- ☐ **ADULT SUPERVISION**
- ☐ Read product labels for use and disposal guidelines.
- ☐ Splash-proof safety goggles
- ☐ Chemical safety gloves
- ☐ **ONLY** mix chemicals as directed.
- ☐ **NEVER** touch dry ice with your bare hands or skin.

ELECTRICAL SOURCES such as batteries:
- ☐ **ONLY** use new, undamaged batteries.
- ☐ **ALWAYS** perform your experiment in a clear, open space far away from any flammable objects and water.

FLAMES AND HEAT SOURCES such as matches, candles, stoves, hot metals, or boiling water:
- ☐ **ADULT SUPERVISION**
- ☐ Keep a fire extinguisher or other fire-safety equipment within reach.
- ☐ Perform activities in a clean, open space away from flammable objects.
- ☐ **DO NOT** wear loose clothes or loose hair.
- ☐ **NEVER** heat flammable liquids. Wear heat-resistant mitts.
- ☐ Place candles in metal drip pans before lighting the flame, and do not remove them until after the flame is extinguished.

ABOUT THIS BOOK

Inside this book you will find activities, mysteries, and projects that take science to extremes!

> WHAT KIND OF EXTREMES?

Extreme temperatures. Not only did we do and shoot the experiments in this book in three separate seasons (winter, spring, and summer), but we experimented with freezing cold, boiling heat, and stuff that depended on all the temperatures in between.

Extreme environments, such as the deep sea where the pressure is much greater than on land.

Extreme abilities, such as animals' power to see beyond the visible (to humans) spectrum of light.

And much more! To create this book, my expert team and I met with three dozen kids, one dog, and several adults (including a mail carrier) to work on experiments and projects, trying and failing and screaming and cooperating and inspiring each other. We made messes. We made art. We made discoveries. And we made this book so that you can experience what we experienced, and more.

We had outstanding successes—Rainy Day Surprise and MYO OOHO were huge hits—as well as quieter ones: The Eco-Cooler and Peeps Zap worked better than we anticipated.

We had fails for reasons outside our control: We tried a Backyard Bioblitz in a yard that had been sprayed for mosquitoes. We had fails for reasons we didn't fully understand: Our first Hero's Engines just wouldn't spin until we figured out the details.

And we came up with fixes that made us all laugh with delight: MYO Digital Microscope and Liquid Lens, for example.

And, once again, we did simple things that turned out to be ooh-awesome, including Color Explosion and Bottle Won't Pour.

As we did all the experiments and projects in this book—really did them, no posing—we explored the limits of what we could do, adding bonus questions, considerations, and extra information and new connections to help you make the most of your try.

Treat this book as a starting point. Science is about trial and error, and discovery happens in situations where the scientist (that's you!) pushes into areas he or she doesn't understand.

Although some of the activities here don't

translate into science fair projects, they do connect with the STEAM goals that are so important in our times—Science, Technology, Engineering, Art, and Math. This time around we're adding art, because it connects science to self-expression, discovery, and communication.

Wishing you extreme good luck and a lot of fun as you try this book.

Full STEAM ahead!

—Karen Romano Young and Matthew Rakola

TRYING NEW THINGS!

Lots of times trying new things made us nervous. Three things helped us feel more confident.

1 **The only rules in this book concern safety.** If you see this symbol, pay attention and be extra careful. Basically, if you're working with appliances, tools, chemicals, electricity, or open flames, you need to have an adult with you and you must take appropriate safety precautions. Get yourself some protective goggles, and use them! **Follow the warnings and advice in the safety check.** Be safe, be smart.

2 **Work with someone else.** As you work through this book, you'll see a **"Who You Need" icon that shows you the fewest people needed** for each project and if you need an adult's help. Grab a few more people. Duplicate materials if necessary, or work with a partner. Two heads really are better than one, especially when things get tricky. As you'll see from our pictures, we think "the more, the merrier"—but we thought it would be useful to show that many of our experiments and projects don't need so many people.

3 **It's OK not to know what you're doing.** It's OK if things go wrong. Get used to it, because trying to fix what goes wrong leads to discoveries and new confidence. The exhilaration we felt when we figured out how to do something—whether it's where to find dry ice in our town, how to adjust a mechanism so that it has power, or what to bait a trap with to lure bugs—was worth the nerves we felt at the beginning. We've learned a lot by putting this book together—including how to make things easier or fix things that go wrong—so **check out the GLITCH and NOTE sections** of the experiments.

MEET OUR SCIENTISTS

ALEX

ANTONIO

ARYA

AUDREY

COLTON

CONNOR

CORI

DANIELA

DAVID

DESIREE

DYLAN

ELECTRA

EMILY

GABRIEL

GABRIELLE

HENRY

JACOB

JAMAI

JAMEER

JOE

JUSTICE

KAMARI

KAMERON

KARISA

KRISTINE

LIAM

MAX

MAYA

MYCHAL-JAEL

MYRRH

NICOLE

RENUKA

SAM

SAMUEL

SAYLA

SOFIA

ROSIE THE DOG

SNOW AND ICE

'T is the season for extreme weather—whether it's winter where you are or not! For some of these projects, you'll need extreme temperatures. But for others, you can make your own cold. *Brrrrrrace* yourself for chilly discovery.

FROZEN BUBBLES
PAGE 16

COOL GLOW STICKS
PAGE 14

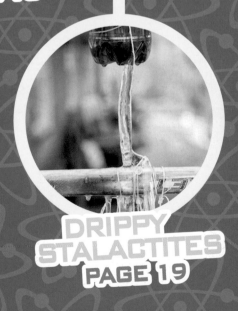

DRIPPY STALACTITES
PAGE 19

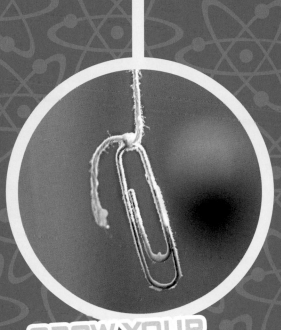

COOL GLOW STICKS

Ice sheds new light on the workings of glow sticks.

SAFETY CHECK

SIMPLE

WHO YOU NEED

JUST YOU

CONCEPTS

THERMODYNAMICS, CHEMISTRY

HOW LONG IT TAKES
10 to 15 minutes

WHAT YOU NEED
glow sticks
a glass of ice water
salt

We heard cold had a weird effect on a familiar item that relies on a chemical reaction—so we decided to see how it worked for us.

INSIDER INFO:
This works best
in a dim room.

WHAT TO DO

1 SNAP THE GLOW STICK. Don't shake it yet. Look at it closely.

2 NOW SHAKE IT. What happens?

3 FILL A GLASS with ice and add some water so it comes about halfway up the ice.

4 ADD A FEW tablespoons of salt to the ice-water mixture.

5 PUT THE GLOW STICK half-way into the ice water.

6 TAKE IT OUT AGAIN. What has happened?

7 TRY WARMING UP the glow stick by rolling it between the palms of your hands. Can you reverse the effect of the ice?

WHAT TO EXPECT Snapping the glow stick and shaking it activates its fluorescence, and cold slows down that reaction.

WHAT'S GOING ON Glow sticks are made of two plastic tubes. The outer one holds the chemical diphenyl oxalate and dye (this is what makes the glow sticks different colors). The inner plastic tube contains hydrogen peroxide. This is the tube that breaks open when you snap the glow stick. The hydrogen peroxide reacts with the diphenyl oxalate to make it fluoresce. The swirls that happen as the glow stick begins to glow show the reaction is happening. The molecules in the reaction move more quickly in warmth than in cold—just like any molecules. But the reactions let you see the different speeds at which they move.

"Would it work if it didn't have salt in it?"
—Jacob

QUESTION THIS!

Will cooling your glow stick make its glow last longer?

"Will a hand warmer recharge it?"
—Antonio

OUR TRY

We didn't know what difference the salt made, so we tried it in a glass of ice water with no salt. It was harder to push the glow stick into the ice, making us think that the salt was actually making the ice softer—so maybe it sped up the effect, making the cold come off the ice faster.

FROZEN BUBBLES

Worth freezing your fingers? We think so.

SAFETY CHECK

SIMPLE

WHO YOU NEED

GRAB A GROWN-UP

SUPERVISION: HOT WATER

CONCEPTS

CHEMISTRY, PHYSICS, FREEZING

> ### HOW LONG IT TAKES
> Make the bubble mixture a day ahead. It can take a few minutes to get a bubble to freeze under the right conditions. Leave frozen bubbles overnight to see how that affects them.

> ### WHAT YOU NEED
> 2 cups hot water (distilled is best)
> ½ cup dish soap
> ½ cup corn syrup
> basket or picture frame (or both)
> bubble wands
> bowl, jar, or pan for soap mixture
> camera
> outdoor thermometer
> OPTIONAL: glow sticks or highlighters; food coloring; containers for mixing different colors of bubble mix; glycerine; Christmas lights

Extremely cold out? Excellent! Temperatures around zero create the perfect conditions for freezing bubbles. Try blowing your bubbles at sundown—and getting up early to see the results at sunrise.

> "What would happen if we froze the bubble wand overnight—would it freeze flat?"
> —Antonio

Extreme
CoLd
Bubbles

4- hot w
1- dawn
1- Karo

INSIDER INFO:
To photograph your frozen bubbles, citizen scientist Gwen Balogh recommends getting up at first light. "It's still super-cold and the natural tint will be rosy or golden—and it makes the frost crystals really show up."

WHAT TO DO

! 1 MAKE BUBBLE MIXTURE by combining hot water, dish soap, and corn syrup. Stir slowly to combine. Try to agitate the mixture as little as possible. Keep in a jar overnight. The mixture seems to work best when it has been allowed to settle overnight. Don't shake it around.

2 USING A BASKET OR PICTURE FRAME, set a base for your bubbles in a sheltered, very cold area. Consider setting up your bubbles at sunset, when the wind dies down and the temperature drops. Think about lighting. You might want to place a string of Christmas lights inside a basket or beneath a picture frame. The light will glitter on your bubbles and make them beautiful—and make it easy for you to see them in a dark spot. But you can also just let the bubbles freeze in the dark and check them with a flashlight, or get up in the morning to see them in the first light!

3 BLOW BUBBLES and try to get them to land on your base. Blow extra because some might pop. Step away from them gently, as any slight motion could cause them to pop, and watch them from afar. (This is why it's great to have lights near them to make them show up.)

Continued on next page

BONUS

Add the contents of a glow stick or the felt from inside a highlighter (break it in half and pull out the felt) to your jar of bubble mixture to make it glow in the dark.

Add food coloring to your bubble mixture to change the color of the bubbles. Consider dividing the bubble mixture into different containers and dyeing them each another color.

NOTE ON BUBBLES
Various bubble recipes are needed throughout this book. I've included the ones that were recommended by people who tried these activities before. Feel free to create your own recipe, to experiment with proportions and measurements, or to switch the recipes around. In this book we also suggest blowing bubbles with your breath, with hot air from a hair dryer, or with helium from a party balloon kit. Foam can be blown with all these and with a shop vacuum, too.

FOR BUBBLES IN THE EXTREME COLD:
4 parts hot water
1 part dish soap
1 part corn syrup

FOR BIG BUBBLES:
5 parts hot water
2 parts dish soap
1 part corn syrup

FOR BUBBLES AT NORMAL TEMPERATURES:
2 parts hot water
1 part dish soap
1 part glycerin (available in a drug store and some grocery stores)

FOR BUBBLE FOAM:
12 parts hot water
4 parts dish soap
1 part glycerin

WHAT TO EXPECT If the air is cold enough, it will freeze the soapy membrane of your bubble.

WHAT'S GOING ON When unfrozen, the bubble membrane is formed of soapy cells that are fragile because any movement affecting one ripples through the rest, causing the membrane to break and the bubble to pop. The cells of soap that form the bubble membrane solidify as they freeze, making the bubble more rigid and less likely to pop.

GLITCH Note that bonus ingredients could affect the chemistry of the bubble mixture and the quality of the bubbles, so experiment!

OUR TRY

• At first the bubbles that landed on the picture frame popped until Jacob got the idea of soaping up the picture frame. We used a bubble wand to splash bubble mix onto it. Once there was bubble mix coating the glass, the bubbles seemed to stick.

• Footsteps on the porch floor can create enough vibrations to pop the bubble, so blow as many as you can to ensure that you have enough to get a frozen bubble to last.

QUESTION THIS!

What happens if you drip a drop of water onto your frozen bubble?

DRIPPY STALACTITES

Icicles hold on tighter than flowing water, reaching toward the ground.

> **HOW LONG IT TAKES**
> All day, on a day 20°F or lower

> **WHAT YOU NEED**
> ladder
> empty bottle (1 liter)
> broom handle or any stick (we used an old hockey stick)
> 6 heavy plastic cups
> baking sheet or tray for base (note that food coloring can stain a floor or patio stones)
> sewing needle (for poking a hole for putting string into the bottle)
> thin string
> scissors
> stool
> water
> pitcher
> food coloring
> water pistol, turkey baster, or anything that will let you direct a flow of water
> OPTIONAL: small piece of sponge or washcloth may be necessary and helpful for directing flow and mopping up drops

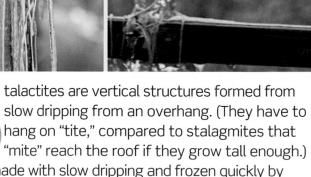

S talactites are vertical structures formed from slow dripping from an overhang. (They have to hang on "tite," compared to stalagmites that "mite" reach the roof if they grow tall enough.) Icicles made with slow dripping and frozen quickly by extreme cold demonstrate this process.

WHAT TO DO

1 SET UP THE ICICLE TOWER. You can use a ladder with steps to support the bottle and stick, with the tray of cups below it. We used garden hooks (they're usually used to hold hanging plants) and string to hang the bottle and our hockey stick. The basic setup is as follows, from top to bottom:

- **a** bottle set or hung from a high point.
- **b** string coming from bottle (step 2) 12 to 24 inches down to the stick
- **c** stick set or hung horizontally 12 to 24 inches below the bottle (step 3)
- **d** strings hanging from the stick 5 feet or more down to cups set on a tray on the ground or floor (step 4)

2 REMOVE THE CAP from the bottle. Use a sewing needle to poke a hole in the side of the empty bottle near the bottom. Put a knot at one end of a length of string and thread it through the bottle so that the knot is inside the bottle. You will tie the other end of the string to the stick about 12 to 24 inches below the bottle.

3 HANG OR PROP A STICK 12 to 24 inches below the bottle. You can suspend it between the two legs of the ladder by setting it across steps or hang it, as we did, from the edge of an overhang, using hooks and/or string.

4 TIE FIVE OR SIX STRINGS from the center of the stick (near the string that goes up to the bottle) so that they descend from the stick to the cups on the ground. These strings should be 5 to 6 feet long. We recommend you tie the tops of the strings at the point where the bottle string is, then lead the opposite end of each string toward a cup. The strings should be long enough to settle into the cups and stay there.

"I wonder if we can get water to drip from the blade of the hockey stick?"
—Maya

5

QUESTION THIS!

What effect does the shape of the stick have on the icicles that result? Does a hockey stick's square shape work better than a stick from a tree? What about texture? Is wood (or a bark-covered stick) a better conductor of water than a slick PVC pipe, or varnished round broomstick?

5 SET UP A STOOL that will allow you to reach the top of your bottle to pour water in.

6 FILL THE BOTTLE with water. Watch what happens as water trickles out of the hole. It SHOULD only trickle. Adjust the flow by making the string knot bigger or packing a piece of sponge or cloth around the hole. The water should flow down the main string, along the stick, and down the lower strings to the cups. The flow should be slow enough that the water on the strings begins to freeze.

7 KEEP POURING and freezing as long as you want. If all goes well you should build a beautiful structure of icicles that can be enjoyed as they are or separated as you wish.

> **TWEAKS AND TWISTS** You can also change the color of the water. If it is cold enough that the icicles don't remelt each time liquid water is added, you'll get ice frozen in different-colored layers, stripes, and ribbons.

> **GLITCH** If your strings are slow to flow, freeze up, or dry out, use a water pistol or baster to trickle additional water down them. Strings will freeze best if left still and soaked well. If it's too warm out—or if the water flows too quickly—icicles may not form. If the water flows too slowly, you can use a water pistol to gently wet the string and keep the ice flowing in a downward direction.

"It's icicling down the string. I think that's the whole point of it."
—Electra

BONUS

Use a smartphone to photograph your icicles as they gradually form. Link the photographs to make a time-lapse file showing the formation of your icicles.

GROW YOUR OWN SNOW

Ultracold + water vapor = crystals (snow!)

SAFETY CHECK

TRICKY

WHO YOU NEED

GRAB A GROWN-UP

SUPERVISION: DRY ICE, HAMMER, KNIFE, SEWING NEEDLE

CONCEPTS

CHEMISTRY, PROPERTIES OF WATER, FREEZING, CRYSTALS, DISTILLATION

HOW LONG IT TAKES
One hour

WHAT YOU NEED
plastic soda bottle, 20-ounce, empty and clean
knife or scissors
sponge
t pins (from a sewing supply or craft store)
sewing needle
thin string (fishing line will also work)
button
paper clip
2 buckets or other containers. One should be smaller and able to accommodate the soda bottle, leaving an inch or two of space around the sides. The other should be larger and able to accommodate the smaller bucket, leaving an inch or two of space around the sides.
insulating material such as towels, newspaper, or shipping peanuts
dry ice—about 5 pounds (see safety tips, p. 7)
hammer to break up the ice if needed
2 plastic bags
SAFETY EQUIPMENT: heavy insulated mittens or gloves with ice protection coating

FROST
forms when water vapor freezes.

SNOW
forms in the clouds as water droplets crystallize.

This experiment comes from Kenneth G. Libbrecht, a physics professor at California Institute of Technology (Caltech), who studied crystal growth. You can imitate his work by building a snow crystal growth chamber (or diffusion chamber) in your kitchen!

DRY ICE is frozen carbon dioxide. Its temperature is around -100°F. Handle it only with insulated mittens or protective gloves, **never with bare hands.**

WHAT TO DO

1 CUT THE BOTTOM 1½ inches off the soda bottle carefully. You will use both portions of the bottle.

2 USING THE BOTTOM of the bottle as a template, cut the sponge so that it fits inside with just a little squishing. Use t pins to fasten the sponge, sticking the pins in from the outside, through the sides of the bottle and into the sponge.

3 THREAD THE SEWING NEEDLE with the string or fishing line and make a knot at one end. Push the needle from the outside of the bottle bottom through the center of the plastic, through the sponge, and pull through. The string or line should be about 12 inches long. (Hint: Our needle made a hole too big for our knot, and the string kept pulling through the sponge and falling out. So we tied one end of the fishing line to a button, then used the needle to push the end through the sponge again. The button kept the line from falling out.) Tie the paper clip to the end of this line. The paper clip will weigh down the string as it hangs.

4 PLACE THE SMALLER BUCKET inside the larger bucket, surrounding its bottom and sides with insulation material.

Continued on next page

SNOW AND ICE

! ▶ 5 HAVE AN ADULT HELP you place dry ice in two plastic bags and carefully break it apart. Pour a layer of dry ice into the smaller bucket. Take the cap off the soda bottle and stand it neck-down in the bucket. Pour dry ice around it until the ice extends halfway up the sides of the bottle.

6 WET THE SPONGE. Place it back in the bottle bottom if you've removed it. Fit the bottle bottom, with sponge inside, on top of the bottle that's in the smaller bucket.

! ▶ 7 ADD EXTRA DRY ICE as needed to keep the temperature cold as the crystals form.

WHAT TO EXPECT Small ice crystals should begin forming after 5 to 10 minutes.

WHAT'S GOING ON
• Dry ice doesn't melt, it sublimes. That is, it changes from a solid to a gas when it is warmed, producing carbon dioxide gas in the process.
• The bottle becomes a diffusion chamber, in which air is chilled at the bottom and warm at the top. This creates the condition in which crystals can grow.
• The water evaporates from the sponge. The water vapor travels around the bottle, until the air inside it gets super-saturated, with humidity at more than 100 percent. Then vapor molecules attach to the string and form a crystal. The string provides a nucleation site where condensation can occur. In the atmosphere, dust crystals perform this purpose! There, supersaturated air condenses into water droplets if the temperature is above 32°F (0°C) and into ice crystals (snow) if the air temperature is below 32°F.

5

6

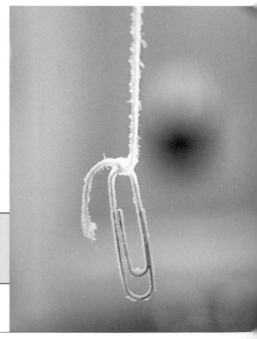

BONUS

Use a smartphone or other camera to photograph ice crystals.

FREEZING IN-TIME

How will the natural world change your art?

CONCEPTS

TIME, SEASON, ENVIRONMENTAL CHANGES, TIDES, WIND, WEATHER

> ### HOW LONG IT TAKES
> An hour or longer to construct a sculpture, and days or weeks to observe the changes affected by time, tide, and weather changes

> ### WHAT YOU NEED
> natural materials such as stones, pinecones, shells, leaves, sticks, driftwood, seaweed tools and containers to help move water or help it freeze: buckets, spoons, baster, water pistol, pitcher

A ndy Goldsworthy is an artist whose work relies on the passage of time in the natural world. We let him inspire us as we built cold-weather sculptures and experimented on snow and ice. Let us inspire you to try your own extreme art.

INSIDER INFO:
Andy Goldsworthy is a world-renowned and beloved artist who creates sculptures out of natural objects. His artwork is designed to look different in different lights and under different conditions, including high and low tide. Often his artwork is designed to change or fall apart physically as a chill thaws, the wind blows, or water carries things away.

SNOW AND ICE

!

WHAT TO DO

1 TAKE A LOOK AROUND you and determine what will change. Light? Tide? Wind? Ice, snow, or water? Build a sculpture or design a picture that will change with these conditions.

2 Consider these options:

- **a** Build a tower using stones, shells, seaweed, leaves, grass, or whatever you can find. Use a baster or water pistol to inject water among the natural objects, supporting them carefully as they freeze. What will happen as the tower freezes and thaws?

- **b** Build such a tower on the beach or on a jetty at low tide. Think about what will happen to it as the tide comes in. How will it change? Will it stay up or collapse?

- **c** Find a puddle. If it's frozen, add natural elements to the ice, creating a design. If you want, add water to freeze your design in place. Return to your artwork, observing it as conditions change. If the water in your puddle is liquid, add natural elements to it, building them up to the water level so they can be seen. Return to the artwork as the puddle freezes, checking it and observing the change.

- **d** Create a design on a beach and monitor it as wind and tide alter it.

> **WHAT TO EXPECT** Small ice crystals should begin forming after 5 to 10 minutes.

> **GLITCH** Stuff falls over. Art gets destroyed by wind or waves. Make that a part of your plan. Roll with the natural changes, and let them inspire you to new shapes and forms.

OUR TRY

- Maya and Electra used ice chunks cut from the edge of one pond to build a structure on the frozen surface of another pond. Their sculpture had shelves for three pine-cones—like walruses on an ice floe. They used water pistols to make ice that froze their ice blocks to one another.
- Jacob scraped and punched a pattern in the ice of the pond using a stick, then poured hot water on it to make the holes more pronounced.
- Antonio scratched his name in the ice.
- Jacob and Antonio used ice chunks to build an "ice palace" atop a little hillock of ferns along the small pond.
- We made a daisy sculpture on top of a floating chunk of ice, using iris grasses, pine cones, and dead flowers. The ice froze over, embedding the daisy design in the ice. Later the ice melted beneath it and it sank a little. A day later a shower of snow coated it. Then the pond froze again and it froze into the ice, sunken in somewhat. What surprised us was that it never moved, seeming to be in an area of the pond where the water just wasn't going anywhere.

BONUS

Most artwork serves to freeze a moment in time, so what happens when the artwork is designed to change with time, tide, or temperature? Andy Goldsworthy considers photographs and videos of his changing artwork to be important parts of displaying the artwork itself. You can, too. Make it Goldsworthy-worthy.

SUMMER SNOWBALL

Build a giant snowball—as big as will fit into your freezer.

"The snow isn't 'packing snow.' How 'packing' it is depends on the water. There isn't enough water in it to hold together."
—Kristine

SAFETY CHECK

SIMPLE

WHO YOU NEED

JUST YOU

CONCEPTS

THERMODYNAMICS, WEATHER EFFECTS, CHEMISTRY

> **HOW LONG IT TAKES**
> An hour to build the snowball; decide for yourself how long you will freeze it before allowing it to melt

> **WHAT YOU NEED**
> snow
> cloth or plastic measuring tape
> notebook and pen
> treasures:
>   small natural items
>   messages written on paper and then taped over with transparent tape, sealed in plastic bags, or laminated
>   little toys, metal or plastic objects, especially a plastic woolly mammoth or dinosaurs— whatever won't melt or disintegrate
> large freezer space

What's more fun than planning to bring a snowball out of the freezer in July? Predicting how fast it will melt to reveal buried treasure.

SNOW AND ICE

1

2

3

1 MAKE A SMALL SNOW-BALL. Measure its circumference with the measuring tape. Embed one of your treasures in its outer rim. (Keep a list of prizes and the order in which you add them to your snowball.)

2 ENLARGE THE SNOWBALL by packing snow on or rolling it through the snow to hide the first treasure. Add a treasure to this layer.

3 CONTINUE ADDING LAYERS and treasures. Before you add each treasure, measure the circumference of the snowball.

4 CONTINUE TO ADD LAYERS of snow and treasures until either (a) you're out of treasures or (b) you're out of snow or (c) you're out of space in your freezer. Place the snowball in the freezer.

4

5 **WAIT** a few hours and bring the snowball out into a bathtub—or wait months and months for a warm, sunny day to take your snowball out of the freezer.

6 **PREDICT HOW LONG** it will take for each treasure to come to light as the snowball melts.

7 **OBSERVE PEOPLE'S** reactions as the snowball melts and the secret objects emerge.

> GLITCH Some things don't work well embedded in a snowball. We discovered a few items that just wouldn't stay in, so we abandoned them. You can always add things from your junk drawer or coat pocket, or just natural objects.

5

BONUS

Make a list of your treasures and the circumference measurements at which they were embedded in the snow. Ask friends and family to bet on how long it will take the snowball to melt to each prize. Keep a chart of this: The one who guesses correctly takes home the prize!

"The fortune cookie has air in the bag so the snow is just falling off and the noisemaker is too big and didn't want to go in. It was a waste of time, basically."
—Nicole

SURVIVAL SKILLS

Survive these science challenges and you may equip yourself with handy skills for future situations. Along the way learn what it takes to get clean drinking water, shine a brighter light, and even adapt your phone into a new kind of tool.

PURE, SWEET WATER

SURVIVAL STILL

ICE CANDLE

FIRE-STARTER ICE
PAGE 38

MYO DIGITAL MICROSCOPE
PAGE 43

ORANGE OIL LAMP
PAGE 41

SURVIVAL STILL

A solar still can be used to purify water in an extreme environment.

SAFETY CHECK

SIMPLE	WHO YOU NEED
	JUST YOU

SUPERVISION: COLLECTING OUTDOOR WATER SAMPLE

CONCEPTS

CHEMISTRY, CONDENSATION, DISTILLATION

HOW LONG IT TAKES
Setup: 15 minutes (not including time to gather water)
Outcome: one day to three weeks

WHAT YOU NEED
bowl
coffee cup that is shorter than the rim of the bowl
water
plastic wrap
a small rock
OPTIONAL: water test kit

Under certain conditions, water vapor changes to liquid water. What does it take to create those conditions—and how can this process be used to provide clean water? Find out here!

DISTILLATION

is one way of purifying water. In distillation, water is heated and the condensation that forms is gathered, leaving the contaminants behind in the pot. The steam is cooled and liquefies as pure water.

WHAT TO DO

1 FIND AN AREA INSIDE where there's a lot of sun and where your water solar still won't be disturbed for as long as two weeks. Set up your still here.

2 TO MAKE THE STILL, set a cup inside a bowl.

3 FILL THE BOWL with the water you want to purify. Don't let the water spill into the cup. Keep the water level below the rim of the cup.

4 STRETCH PLASTIC WRAP across the bowl with the water and cup inside.

5 SET THE ROCK ATOP the plastic wrap above the cup.

WHAT TO EXPECT Over time—days to weeks—the sun will condense the water into vapor that forms on the inside of the plastic wrap. The weight of the stone will force the wrap down over the cup, so that the clear, pure vapor drips into the cup.

WHAT'S GOING ON The water in the cup shouldn't have any impurities because the impurities won't evaporate from the impure water. The water's impurities will stay in the bowl. Do not drink the water in case some impurities remain.

GLITCH While moving one of our stills from the kitchen to the sunny windowsill, we must have splashed pond water into the coffee cup, contaminating it. It's better not to try to transport the still.

BONUS

Test the water with the kit. Use a professional water test kit to assess your water's purity. Some kits involve tapes coated with chemicals that react with your water to give you information about its purity, pH, and other characteristics. For another kind of kit, see p. 34, Pure, Sweet Water.

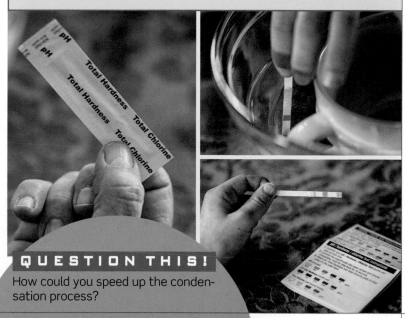

QUESTION THIS!

How could you speed up the condensation process?

PURE, SWEET WATER

Don't have weeks to wait for water? Filter it with natural elements—or your shirt.

SAFETY CHECK

SIMPLE

WHO YOU NEED

GRAB A FRIEND

SUPERVISION: COLLECTING OUTDOOR WATER SAMPLE

CONCEPTS

PROPERTIES OF WATER, SOLIDS AND LIQUIDS, FILTERING PROPERTIES OF MATERIALS, BACKWOODS SKILLS

HOW LONG IT TAKES
30 to 60 minutes, not counting time to find materials

WHAT YOU NEED
tree bark that is flexible enough to shape into a funnel
rubber band or string
grass
pebbles
sand
charcoal or charred firewood
water and containers, one each to pour and catch water in as it filters
OPTIONAL: water tester pen, eyedropper, microscope and slides

PURIFIED WATER
is water from which impurities (contaminants, including minerals and bacteria) have been removed or reduced significantly.

Impure water is a problem for much of the world, and inventions that simply, cheaply purify drinking water have the potential to do great good. Try some water purification materials with us—or come up with and test others you think of yourself.

FILTERED WATER
is water that has been poured through materials that will react with or gather the contaminants, removing them from the water. If your water has lethal bacteria in it, filtering is not going to save your life, but it will clean some solids out of the water and make it clearer.

WHAT TO DO

1 USE BIRCH or another flexible tree bark to form a funnel with a small opening at the bottom, shaping it with your hands. Ask a helper to fasten it with string or a rubber band.

2 LAYER THE INSIDE of the funnel with grass or pebbles first, then sand, then charcoal or charred firewood, then more grass or pebbles.

3 SLOWLY POUR WATER to be purified through the wide end of the funnel, letting it trickle through the layers and out the small bottom opening.

WHAT TO EXPECT The water will pass through the filter materials and drip, somewhat purified, into a clean container below.

WHAT'S GOING ON As water flows or drips through or between the different filtration materials, solids in the water—mud, sand, and organic material like algae and bacteria—are caught. The water that comes out is clearer and cleaner, **but not necessarily clean enough to drink!**

GLITCH If you want purified water, boiling isn't enough. The contaminants have higher boiling temperatures than the water. So after the water is boiled, the contaminants can still be in the water.

1-2

3

QUESTION THIS!

Would filtering the water make it cleaner?

BONUS SUPERVISION: BOILING WATER

Have an adult help you boil water or use a commercial water purifier, which may be a tablet you mix in, an ultraviolet light instrument you shine, or an appliance or water bottle with a special filter to pour the water through. Compare them.

Assess the purity of your water:

- Use a water dropper to place a drop on a microscope slide. Examine your water and see if you can categorize objects you see in it. How do different types of water compare?

- Use a professional water test kit to assess your water's purity.

- Some kits involve tapes coated with chemicals that react with your water to give you information about its purity, pH, and other characteristics. Another commercial water tester uses light to do a digital reading giving similar information. You can see how your water did!

ICE CANDLE

Here's an ice way to get a little more light on the subject.

CONCEPTS

PHYSICS, LIGHT REFRACTION AND REFLECTION, PROPERTIES OF ICE

HOW LONG IT TAKES

3 to 4 hours (including freezing time)

WHAT YOU NEED

metal or glass bowl
water
paper cup
rock
freezer
cutting board
tealight candle (see safety tips, p. 7)

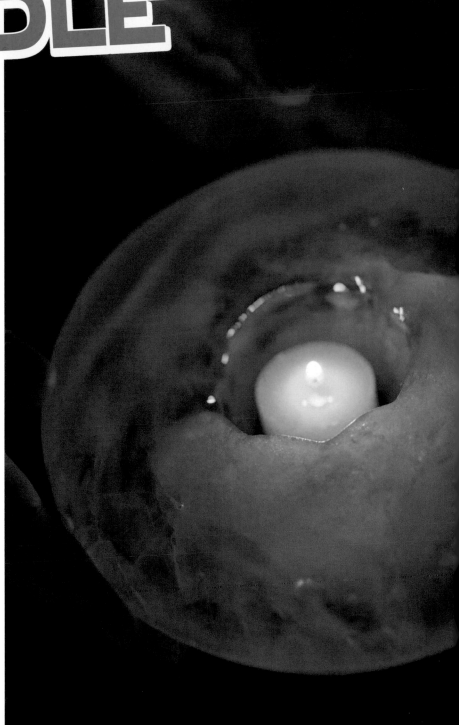

Try this on for size—and try it in any size. We think these ice candles are beautiful as well as useful. What shapes will work? Try a variety, making predictions about the effect each shape will produce.

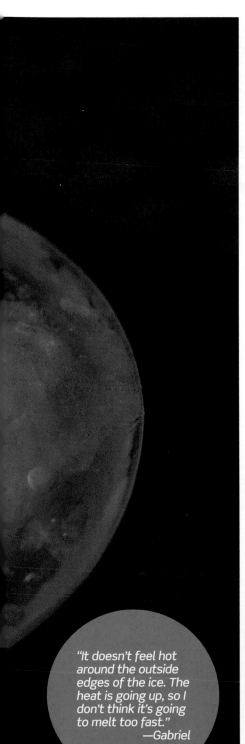

WHAT TO DO

1 FILL A BOWL one or two inches with water, and freeze.

2 SET A PAPER CUP on the ice. Place a rock or other weighted item inside the cup and fill the bowl with more water, not going higher than the edge of the cup. Freeze.

3 REMOVE THE BOWL of ice from the freezer. Tear out the paper cup.

4 FLIP THE BOWL onto the cutting board. Rub your hands over the outside of the bowl to warm it so the ice will drop out.

5 INSERT THE TEALIGHT CANDLE in the hole from the paper cup and light it.
WARNING: *Never leave a flame unattended!*

WHAT TO EXPECT The ice will create a lamp that is brighter than the candle would be on its own.

WHAT'S GOING ON The ice forms a glassy surface that reflects (bounces) and refracts (spreads) the candlelight.

GLITCH Ice cracks or breaks? You can refreeze a cracked or chipped piece of ice by adding water and refreezing. The ice will heal.

QUESTION THIS!

How does the ice affect the light? As a comparison, light another tealight candle nearby. What's the difference between the light projected by the candles?

BONUS

Here's something we didn't try: floating ice candles. But you can.

"It doesn't feel hot around the outside edges of the ice. The heat is going up, so I don't think it's going to melt too fast."
—Gabriel

FIRE-STARTER ICE

Make an ice lens and set it to "singe."

CONCEPTS

OPTICS, LENSES, PRINCIPLES OF LIGHT, IGNITION

> **HOW LONG IT TAKES**
> About an hour once you have ice, longer if you include the time it takes to freeze a chunk of ice (12 to 24 hours, depending on the temperature outside or in your freezer)

> **WHAT YOU NEED**
> a clear, solid chunk of ice 6 to 8 inches square and 3 to 4 inches thick (the larger, the better. More ice = more light = better chance of igniting tinder)
> 2 bowls or cooking pots—one for freezing ice, one for tinder
> tinder: shredded newspaper or paper towels, or hay
> OPTIONAL: cutting board, pitcher of water, water tap (faucet)

Here's one that didn't quite hit its objective of setting something afire for us. Our lenses could be used to redirect light and focus it—and we could see how another try (maybe yours) might achieve the desired result—combustion!

WHAT TO DO

1 MAKE OR FIND a block of ice. Use clear lake or pond ice, or use clean water to fill a pot or bowl. See dimensions in the materials list. Your chunk of ice needs to be as clear as possible and free of bubbles and holes.

! 2 SHAPE THE CHUNK of ice into a lens that is circular in shape and that has convex sides—curved outward uniformly. Here are some options for shaping the lens. (You may come up with others yourself.)

- **a** Use the heat of your hand to melt the ice lens smooth and to shape it.
- **b** Use warm or cold water to shape the lens.

Continued on the next page

"If you can't change it, work with it."
—Nicole

SURVIVAL SKILLS

3 **FILL** a cooking pot with tinder.

4

! 4 EXPERIMENT WITH FOCUSING sunlight through the lens onto the tinder. How can you use the ice lens to bend and direct the light most strongly? Focus the brightest spot of light on the tinder (but don't let ice droplets fall on it). Tinder may smoke first, then light.

GLITCH What if your tinder doesn't light? This shows that your lens is not perfect. But if you can get a stronger, brighter light with one angle through the lens, you are on the right track—and should consider it a success.

QUESTION THIS!

Why would the lens work better if we could achieve a convex shape?

"It might work if you could get the lenses to not melt so fast—so maybe next time we would take the lenses outside to shape them."
—Joe

OUR TRY

Colton and Joe used warm water and their hands to shape the lenses. We set up shredded newspaper in a skillet on the dining room table in the sun, and worked on getting the lenses to focus white stars of bright light on the newspaper. Colton had the idea of placing the ice in a metal sieve so it could be held without melting. The sieve seemed to make the light going through the ice brighter, but it was still hard to hold focus. We tried to use both lenses together—Colton holding his in the sunlight behind Joe's so the light would shine through them together. A valiant effort!

"Oh my gosh, it's bright! I'm going to light the end of this paper."
—Colton

ORANGE OIL LAMP

What a way to glow!

> **HOW LONG IT TAKES**
> 2 or 3 days

> **WHAT YOU NEED**
> paring knife, scout knife, or other sharp,
> easy-to-control knife
> an orange (or two)
> small bowl or saucer
> olive oil
> matches (see safety tips, p. 7)

In this demonstration, an orange's stem—the same structure that conducts water into the fruit—can be used to wick, or absorb and carry, oil to a flame. The structure of the stem—and your ability to shape it carefully—makes the difference.

"It smells like an orange-scented candle."
—Cori

WHAT TO DO

! 1 CUT YOUR ORANGE in half carefully around its "waist" (some say "equator"), but be careful not to cut all the way through the center. Your mission here is to keep the stem at the center of the orange intact and remove the fruit around it.

! 2 SLICE THE ORANGE again, this time from its waist to the hole, or center-bottom of the orange, not the end where the orange attaches to the tree by its stem. When done slicing, remove the skin off the "bottom" half of the orange.

! 3 ONCE YOU'VE REMOVED the skin from the bottom half of the orange, use your knife to carefully remove the fruit from around the stem in this half.

4 CAREFULLY REMOVE the fruit from around the stem inside the skin of the other half. Your goal is to have a hollowed-out orange half with the stem still intact.

5 LET YOUR ORANGE(S) DRY OUT overnight or for two days if you want. We found that the candle works better this way, but try lighting one right away if you want.

6 SET THE EMPTY ORANGE DOWN in a bowl and fill it with olive oil to about ½ inch below the waist of the orange or below the tip of the stem, whichever is lower.

! 7 LIGHT the wick (the stem).

> WHAT TO EXPECT Your dry stem will wick oil up to fuel the flame.

QUESTION THIS!

What factors help this lamp to light? If it doesn't light, what could you do differently?

> WHAT'S GOING ON Capillary action in the orange stem pulls water and nutrients up from the ground into the tree and from the tree into the fruit while the orange is growing. The same mechanism will work to pull oil through the fruit to make your candle. In capillary action, fluid flows from a wet area into a dry one because liquid molecules are drawn to solid molecules on the inside of the stem in a process called adhesion (adhering—sticking to—the walls of the stem).

> GLITCH We did this project with two different kinds of oranges but photographed only one. The first kind of orange—big navel oranges—had bigger, thicker, more intact stems. The second kind (shown in Matt's photographs) had thinner, more breakable stems—but they worked just as well if not better. Try it with a couple of different oranges to see what will work best.

OUR TRY

Kameron, Justice, and Kamari made the candles, and Cori and Liam tested them out. Of our two longest-lasting candles, one stayed lit for two hours; the other, three hours. After that, the wicks burned down to the surface of the olive oil, so the rate of absorption of the oil didn't match the burning rate of the stem. We wondered if tweaking the time we dried out the stem might make it burn longer— maybe if we let it dry for less time. But the candles we lit right away without drying at all didn't stay lit.

3

4

6

7

"Why is this so hard to light? Because it's an orange! It's warm! It works!"
—Liam

MYO DIGITAL MICROSCOPE

Use a smartphone and simple materials to make an effective microscope

> ### HOW LONG IT TAKES
> One hour

> ### WHAT YOU NEED
> scissors
> "self-healing" craft cutting board or kitchen cutting board
> several sheets of cardboard
> 4 pencils
> clear, flat sheet of plastic from packaging, approximately 4 x 6 inches (We used a piece of plastic from a box of greeting cards.)
> clear packing tape
> cheap laser pointer (all you need this for is the lens)
> small, short flashlight
> 8 binder clips big enough to clamp a pencil
> smartphone
> OPTIONAL: X-Acto knife, heavy aluminum foil, white paper

Why build your own microscope? Because it will give you a better understanding of what microscopes do and how they work. And because it'll give you an opportunity to use a smartphone's camera abilities to view things usually too small for your (and the phone's) eye.

WHAT TO DO

1 CUT THREE PIECES of cardboard 7 x 7 inches for the platforms.

2 STACK THE THREE platforms so that the corners are all trued (lined up evenly.) Measure in ¾ inch from each corner to draw an x in the same spot on each corner.

3 WITH ADULT SUPERVISION, use a scissor point to cut through the four x's on each platform. You want the x's to stack right on top of each other when the platforms are stacked so that a pencil in each corner will pass through all three platforms.

4 IN THE MIDDLE PLATFORM, cut a rectangular hole 3 x 5 inches for the stage. Trim your plastic packaging sheet and tape it to the platform.

5 REMOVE THE LENS from a laser pointer.

6 IN THE TOP PLATFORM, cut a round hole to fit the lens. Wedge the lens into the hole.

7 IN THE BOTTOM PLATFORM, cut a round hole to hold your small flashlight in place. It should shine up through the platform to light the object you place there, and it should be positioned under the hole for the lens.

8 ASSEMBLE THE THREE platforms into a tower, pushing a pencil up through the three holes in each corner so that the erasers are on the bottom and the microscope rests on them.

9 USE BINDER CLIPS to hold the platforms at the level you want, and to stabilize the tower structure.

10 SET THE CAMERA LENS of your phone over the laser lens on the top platform. Turn the camera application on.

11 SET THE FLASHLIGHT in the hole on the bottom platform and turn it on. Shine it up through the plastic stage.

12 TEST THE MICROSCOPE with a coin placed on the stage. Adjust your camera's zoom, change the level of the stage, move the light, until you see a clear, magnified image.

13 TRY THE MICROSCOPE using any object you like.

OPTIONAL: Use aluminum foil on the bottom platform to reflect the light. Use white paper (lined if you want a good reference point for size) atop the plastic on the stage to diffuse the light from the flashlight—or cover the flashlight with white paper, using a rubber band or tape to hold it.

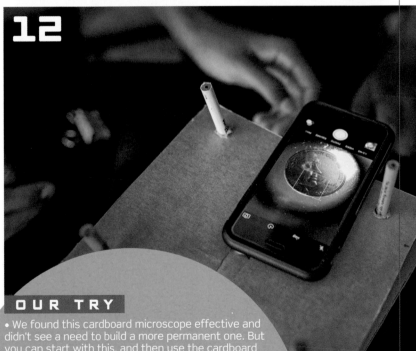

> **WHAT TO EXPECT** Your microscope will magnify your object about double.

> **WHAT'S GOING ON** The lens used to focus the light in the laser, combined with the zoom function on the smartphone, provides the magnification.

> **TWEAKS AND TWISTS** Our first cardboard microscope followed the plans for a wooden version in which the stage (a middle platform smaller than the top and bottom platforms) had supports on only two corners. When Kamari, Kameron, and Justice made theirs, they changed the stage design; instead of connecting on only the front corners, it was the same size as the top and bottom stages, so that the pencils passed through four corners, not just two. They felt that this made for a sturdier microscope.

OUR TRY

• We found this cardboard microscope effective and didn't see a need to build a more permanent one. But you can start with this, and then use the cardboard one as a template for a wooden one, in which pencils and binder clips are replaced with bolts and nuts and the plastic stage is replaced with a sheet of Plexiglass. Why not just give precise measurements for the wooden one and start there? Because then you miss the learning experience that comes with building the cardboard microscope—figuring out the function of each part and the way the parts relate to each other.

• We tried coins, hair, leaves, grass. We also brought a worm in from outside and placed it on our stage, then took a video of its movements. Worked great!

QUESTION THIS!

What would happen if you used additional lenses?

FEEL THE FORCE

Do you work well under pressure? You'll find out with this set of experiments, designed to get you feeling a variety of forces as you play around with the power of playground equipment, your own muscles, and even the air around you.

MINIATURE MARSHMALLOW GETS SMALLER
PAGE 50

THAT SINKING FEELING
PAGE 48

AIR MONSTER
PAGE 55

MERRY-GO-ROUND CATCH
PAGE 52

MAGIC ARMS
PAGE 58

THAT SINKING FEELING

How a submarine, a Styrofoam cup, or a marshmallow feels at the bottom of the sea

CONCEPTS

PRESSURE, DEEP-SEA ENVIRONMENT, PROPERTIES OF FOAM INCLUDING SYNTACTIC FOAM AND STYROFOAM

HOW LONG IT TAKES
20 to 40 minutes

WHAT YOU NEED
cork
thin knife
2-liter plastic soda bottle
mini-marshmallows
bike pump
SAFETY EQUIPMENT: goggles

Syntactic foam—the skin of a deep-diving submarine—allows a submarine to withstand the pressure of the deep sea. See how it works by experimenting with marshmallows—another kind of foam.

2

! 1 MAKE A HOLE in the cork to fit the bike pump needle.

2 HALF FILL the bottle with mini-marshmallows.

! 3 BE SURE YOUR AREA IS CLEAR, then put the cork on the bottle, and pump air into the bottle.

! 4 WHAT HAPPENS to the marshmallows under pressure? What happens when you remove the bike pump? **WARNING:** *The cork can blow, so wear goggles and watch out! (Our cork stayed attached to the bicycle pump, but it still popped loudly and surprisingly.)*

> **TWEAKS AND TWISTS** We drew faces on the marshmallows because we hoped it would help us see their shrinkage and expansion more easily. It did!
> We redid this one because we had the wrong pin for the bicycle pump at first.

3

OUR PREDICTION

Myrrh: "Marshmallows will shrink."
Jameer: "Marshmallows will float."
Jamai: "Marshmallows will get bigger."
Who do you think was right?

4

"They aged but then they got young again."
—Jameer, watching the marshmallows contract and wrinkle, then expand and grow smooth again

OUR TRY

We repeated this experiment twice to see how much we could get the marshmallows to contract under pressure. The first time, it took nine pumps to pop the cork. The second time, it took six pumps.

MINIATURE MARSHMALLOW GETS SMALLER

See the effect of deep-sea pressure on just one marshmallow!

SAFETY CHECK

SIMPLE

WHO YOU NEED

JUST YOU

CONCEPTS

PRESSURE, DEEP-SEA ENVIRONMENT, PROPERTIES OF FOAM INCLUDING SYNTACTIC FOAM AND STYROFOAM

HOW LONG IT TAKES
5 minutes

WHAT YOU NEED
thin marker
plastic syringe **(without needle)** to fit mini-marshmallows
mini-marshmallows

With help from a syringe (without the needle!), you can create pressure that's stronger than the atmosphere, in the palm of your hand.

1

"Whoa! It's shrinking—it looks like it's being sucked in from inside."
—Max

"It's hard to push it in because of the pressure. There's air pushing it out."
—Daniela

"This marshmallow has seven other brothers, though. He'll hardly be missed."
—Dylan, squishing a marshmallow in a syringe.

WHAT TO DO

1 DRAW A FACE or letter on the marshmallow. (This will help you see how it changes under pressure.)

2 PULL THE PLUNGER of the syringe all the way out, and insert a marshmallow. Replace the plunger.

3 SUCK OUT THE AIR by pulling the plunger. Observe the results.

4 PUSH THE PLUNGER BACK IN. Observe the results.

WHAT'S GOING ON The marshmallow may look solid, but it's actually full of air pockets—a foam. When you pump air in, you increase the pressure on the marshmallows and the air inside them is compressed. When air rushes back in, the marshmallows may get larger—and if you suck it out they may get smaller.

KAREN'S TRY

How much pressure is there under the deep-sea? Enough to shrink a regular-size Styrofoam coffee cup with the cover of *Try This!* on it! That's me showing the result of that experiment: a miniature cup with all the air squeezed out. This tiny cup was once a standard-size cup made of Styrofoam (another name for expanded polystyrene foam)—bubbles of polystyrene. While I worked aboard Exploration Vessel *Nautilus*, I drew the *Try This!* cover on this cup, and then we sent it to the bottom of the Caribbean Sea on the remotely operated submersible *Argus*. Under the pressure of the ocean, the polystyrene bubbles were pressed together, shrinking the cup. ROV technician Clancy Emanuel made the bracket (with the yellow National Geographic frame!) that carried the cup to the bottom of the sea aboard *Hercules*.

QUESTION THIS!

Would the weight of the Styrofoam cups (or marshmallows) change under pressure?

MERRY-GO-ROUND CATCH

Can you play catch on a curve?

SAFETY CHECK

DIFFICULT

WHO YOU NEED

GRAB SOME FRIENDS

CONCEPTS

PHYSICS, MOTION, FORCE, CENTRIPETAL FORCE, AND CENTRIFUGAL FORCE.

HOW LONG IT TAKES
15 to 30 minutes

WHAT YOU NEED
playground merry-go-round
ball (use a soft Nerf-like or light, air-filled ball)
at least four ballplayers, plus additional
people to push the merry-go-round

Experiment with the laws of motion as you attempt an activity that looks simple—until you try it. How many factors will you have to manage and control in order to succeed?

"You need to throw a leading pass—ahead of the person so that when he gets to it, it can be caught by him."
—Dylan

WHAT TO DO

1 TWO BALLPLAYERS SIT on the merry-go-round, facing each other. One will be moving forward and the other backward as the merry-go-round spins clockwise.

2 PLAY CATCH before the merry-go-round starts.

3 A PUSHER SETS the merry-go-round spinning. The ballplayers play catch again. What happens if you're the person in the front? What happens if you're the person in the back? How do you have to change the way you throw and catch in order to play successfully without missing?

4 ADD BALLPLAYERS.
Experiment with passing the ball by tossing it forward and back as the merry-go-round spins.

Continued on next page

QUESTION THIS!

• How does the game change as you push faster or slower?

• How do you have to change your throwing and catching in order to not miss?

• What happens if you play catch across the merry-go-round rather than front to back?

• What other variations can you come up with?

FEEL THE FORCE

WHAT TO DO

> > WHAT TO EXPECT Basically, the ball will probably not do what you expect!

> > WHAT'S GOING ON Centrifugal force isn't a true physical force. Instead, it's an impression, a perception of the way something feels rather than what is actually happening— it's a pseudo-force (a fake force). You could compare it to the effect you get when sitting on a train in a station, seeing another train moving and thinking mistakenly that your own train is moving.

So what happens when you feel you're throwing straight but the merry-go-round is turning? Is the ball spinning out or in? Why is it so hard to catch? We tried to throw toward the center of the merry-go-round to compensate for the sense that the ball was being pushed away from the center. But in fact it was not being pushed outward; it was continuing in a straight line. But because we were traveling on a curve, we were experiencing pseudo-force.

OUR TRY

We tried throwing from the ground to the merry-go-round, playing catch in pairs, playing catch in four, facing each other two segments apart and throwing across. We tried throwing high in the air and throwing directly. It was all harder than we thought it would be. The balls went all over the place, everybody missed a lot—much more often than not. People mostly didn't get too dizzy— although photographer Matt had to take a moment to get his bearings after finally getting off! (See if you can figure out where he was positioned while taking these pictures and you'll understand why.)

"Does the fact that you're dizzy throw off your aim?"
—Daniela

"It went the opposite way from what you expected. It had something to do with centrifugal force."
—Dylan

"It was hard. You had to think about where you were throwing it."
—Max

AIR MONSTER

This construction has the potential to blow people away!

Ask people to predict what your (flat) sculpture will look like inflated. It's the same thing you'll have to do as you design and build it.

FEEL THE FORCE

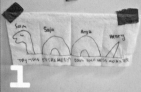

1

2

4

WHAT TO DO

1 USE A PERMANENT MARKER to draw the design for your air monster on your plastic bag. Optional: draw it on paper first, then cut out the paper and use it as a pattern. Trace around the pattern with your marker.

! 2 CUT THROUGH both layers of the plastic bag to cut out your monster.

3 KEEP THE LAYERS TOGETHER, edges trued up (even). Use the clear packing tape to tape the edges together in a seam that goes all the way around the upper portion of the monster but leaves the bottom edges open.

4 USE A SMALL FAN to blow into the monster to inflate it. Check for leaks and fix them with tape.

5 ADD DECORATIONS: Use markers or stickers to add facial features; add hair and trim using other materials.

! 6 WITH AN ADULT, take the monster to a subway grating. Use duct tape to attach the bottom to the grating.

> **WHAT TO EXPECT** Your monster should lie like any limp plastic bag on top of the grating until air vents up. Then it should inflate and stand in place on the grating, surprising passersby.

> **WHAT'S GOING ON** Rising warm air from the vent or fan inflates the sculpture.

> **GLITCH** Our glitch came from the features we wanted to add to create more drama. Arya tied on a bow made of a streamer. Sayla made a bow on top of the hump with two different colors of tape. Samuel added a tongue with streamers, and he and Henry both tried streamers inside their pieces, but this didn't work. The streamers would stream up on the wind and then fall back down and get plastered onto the fan. In the end they put the streamers on the outside and taped them. We concluded that in order to keep them blowing up, not down, we would need to cut a hole in the top of the tube—but we didn't want to do this because then the sculpture might not have inflated as well. Another time, we would test this!

> **TWEAKS AND TWISTS** Add adhesive eyes or googly eyes, plastic or paper streamers, balloons, tissue, yarn, or other materials to create hair, fringe, claws, etc.

"Something's about to happen. I don't know what, but I'm going to watch to see what these people are up to!"
—Passerby

"It's not the right kind of vent, sadly."
—Henry

INSIDER INFO: Observe your subway grating before planning to use it. You're looking for the kind that vents a blast of warm air when the subway passes below. This air will inflate your air monster. Seek out a subway grating that will be noticeable to people but will not obstruct their path. (We're not looking for trouble.)

MAGIC ARMS

1-3

What happens when you store up your own energy?

SAFETY CHECK

SIMPLE	WHO YOU NEED
	GRAB A FRIEND

CONCEPTS

PHYSIOLOGY, ANATOMY, ENERGY, KINETIC MOVEMENT

HOW LONG IT TAKES
2 minutes per person

WHAT YOU NEED
a doorway narrow enough to allow you to stand in it with your hands pressed against the sides (see picture)
stopwatch or smartphone stopwatch app

This muscle-builder never disappoints people who haven't tried it before. Once you've done it, you're in the know; then it's up to you to introduce it to your friends and family!

WHAT TO DO

1 STAND IN THE DOORWAY with your hands hanging down at your sides.

2 KEEPING YOUR ARMS STRAIGHT, press the backs of your hands against the inside of the doorjambs, one on each side.

3 WHILE A FRIEND TIMES YOU, press as hard as you can with your hands for a full 60 seconds.

4 WHEN THE MINUTE IS UP, step out of the doorway into an open area and relax.

> **WHAT TO EXPECT** Your arms will float up above your head. You'll have a feeling that they are lifting themselves without your input. It will be hard to keep them down at first!

> **WHAT'S GOING ON** You use your muscles to energize your arms, but because you're pressing your arms against the doorway, the energy has nowhere to go. After you step out of the doorway, the energy is still there, so it acts (involuntarily) to lift your arms—the action you had prevented them from doing by pushing the energy against the doorjamb.

OUR TRY

All of us experienced stepping out of the doorway and feeling our arms float up involuntarily. We experimented with different versions of this, trying to press our hands at different angles. Cori tried holding her arms UP and pressing her hands against the door to see if her arms would pull DOWN afterward, but it didn't seem to work. Audrey tried pressing the back of her forearms, not her hands, thinking the arms would go WIDE as well as UP. They did go wider. But the most dramatic variation was bending at the waist while pressing with the back of the hands. Then the arms went up like wings!

"I think it's a placebo effect. It makes you want to lift." —Liam

"Doesn't it feel weird?" —Cori

"Oh! I can feel it! It's like pillows are pushing you up." —Gabriel

ANIMAL SUPERPOWERS

What do a flashlight, a bucket of ice, and a TV remote control have in common? They all can get you looking at life as animals do. Look through their eyes, get under their skins, and have a furry nice time doing it!

USE YOUR DOG'S HAIR AS WOOL
PAGE 64

REINDEER VISION
PAGE 62

SPIN WOOL INTO YARN
PAGE 66

FINGER KNITTING
PAGE 68

BLUBBER GLOVES
PAGE 74

INFRARED INTERFERENCE
PAGE 71

REINDEER VISION

Looking for lichen takes special eyesight.

CONCEPTS

OPTICS, VISION, ADAPTATIONS, CLIMATE, BIOLOGY

HOW LONG IT TAKES
20 to 30 minutes

WHAT YOU NEED
wooded area covered lightly in snow that also has lichens, at dusk or darker morning or evening
ultraviolet flashlight and batteries (see safety tips, p. 7)
OPTIONAL: map of the area (you can make your own)

Vision is one of the physical abilities that can change as an animal adapts to its environmental niche—the food it requires, or the predators that are after it. Use technology to borrow animal eyesight and see if you can find food.

Jacob: *"Do reindeer really exist?"*

Maya: *"How else do you think Santa gets here?"*

OUR TRY

We explored the woods at
sundown. As it became darker we
shone our UV flashlights on lichens
along the pines and back pond and
found some whitish spots, but it
wasn't until we analyzed some
patches of lichens and moss on a
big rock that the UV flashlights
brought out sparkles of blue and
orange fluorescence. We also found
them in our clothes (particularly the
sleeve of Jacob's jacket and some
of the knitted gloves).

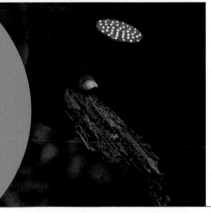

WHAT TO DO

1 IMAGINE that you are a reindeer
using your special ultraviolet vision to find
food under the snow. Use your ultraviolet
flashlight to look for glowing specks of
lichen and moss.

> **WHAT TO EXPECT** The lichen or moss
might simply look whiter or brighter against
their surroundings in the light of your flashlight, but there are some types that will glow
orange, blue, lime green, purple, or pink.
>
> The flashlight may also highlight animal
products such as urine, scat, or fur.

> **WHAT'S GOING ON** Reindeer are the
only mammals with natural ultraviolet vision.
In surroundings covered in white snow that
produces 90 percent ultraviolet light,
humans may experience snow blindness,
eye damage caused by ultraviolet light that
reflects off white snow and "sunburns" our
eyes' corneas and lens. But reindeer have
evolved the ability to see in polar light conditions. Among the things that absorb ultraviolet light, showing up black against the
bright background, are urine and fur—signs
of the herd or of predators—and lichens, the
food reindeer graze on. Because reindeer
can see fur, they're able to spot wolves—
even when the wolves are well-camouflaged
and invisible to other animals.

BONUS

BONUS 1

Ultraviolet flashlights are marketed as
tools for finding the source of a stinky pet
smell. If you're having trouble figuring out
what part of the carpet the puppy peed
on, try an ultraviolet flashlight.

BONUS 2

Once you've located fluorescent materials
(bark, lichens, etc.), how could you create a
map or trail to help others take the tour?
Make your map and hand over the flashlight.
See how many fluorescent objects they can
find—and how many they can add. Reindeer-
antler headbands are strictly optional!

USE YOUR DOG'S HAIR AS WOOL

Dog hair: It's a fashion statement and a scientific tool!

SAFETY CHECK

SIMPLE

WHO YOU NEED

GRAB A GROWN-UP & SOME FRIENDS

SUPERVISION: CAUTION AROUND PETS. DO NOT TRY THIS EXPERIMENT WITH ANY PET THAT SHOWS AGGRESSION. IT MAY BITE.

CONCEPTS

BIOLOGY, PLANTS, ANIMALS, FIBER ARTS, PRINCIPLES OF HAIR AND WOOL

HOW LONG IT TAKES

2 or 3 hours (including time spent washing, drying, and brushing your dog)

WHAT YOU NEED

a long-haired dog such as a golden retriever, a Keeshond, or a Great Pyrenees. Any dog with hair 2 to 4 inches long will do. Shorter than that and the hair will shed out of the yarn—no good!

dog brush or comb for combing your dog's hair

2 flat, pin-type dog brushes or hand carding brushes for carding the dog hair.

NOTE: You can use dog brushes for this. Carding brushes are more expensive. If you go into business spinning dog hair into yarn, you may want to buy hand carding brushes or even a machine called a drum carder. If you know anyone who has a drum carder, you could ask them to card your dog's hair for you.

Sheep do it. So do goats, rabbits, llamas, and alpacas. You may not have realized that certain dog hair can be formed into yarn and used to make knitted textiles. Here's your chance to see how wool works.

CARD used as a verb in this context comes from the Latin word carduus, *which means thistle, or teasel.*

WHAT TO DO

1 BRUSH YOUR DOG. If you want to get a lot of hair—and your dog is losing her coat—it's practical to give her a bath first, then dry her or let her dry. After a wash, brushing will bring out a lot more hair (washing makes the coat drop out) and the dog's hair will be cleaner. Don't try to brush a wet dog! You'll need a big pile of hair, so brush the whole dog.

2 CARD THE HAIR. Place a small wad of hair on one pin-type dog brush or carding brush, and use the other brush to brush it smooth.

3 LIFT THE HAIR OFF the brush in a mat called a rolag. Do this by lifting all the hairs off one edge and rolling the mat of hair as you lift, moving across to the other edge.

4 CONTINUE CARDING WOOL, and when you're ready to remove the next rolag, lay its edge together with the first one. This way you'll be rolling these fibers into one rolag. They might not stick together that well, but spinning will fix that.

ROLAG *Wool fibers that have been carded*

WHAT TO EXPECT Your rolag will be a fuzzy mat with edges that are looser than the middle. Keep a light hand and just keep carding and rolling.

WHAT'S GOING ON The purpose of carding is to get all the fibers in the hair traveling in the same direction. As the two cards or brushes move in opposite directions, they organize the hair fibers, clearing out tangles.

WHAT TO DO NEXT Go on to spin your rolag fibers into yarn (see p. 60, Spin Wool Into Yarn), then knit them into a collar for your dog!

BONUS

A teasel is a plant that can be used to "tease" wool fibers, combing them in one direction. In the old days it was preferred to metal carding tools because the teasel would break if used too roughly, while the woolen fibers would break if the metal tool was used too aggressively. (Better to sacrifice the plant than the wool!)

SPIN WOOL INTO YARN

Use gravity and a Stone Age tool to create yarn out of wool—from a sheep or your dog

SAFETY CHECK

DIFFICULT

WHO YOU NEED

GRAB A GROWN-UP

SUPERVISION: DROP SPINDLE, SCISSORS

CONCEPTS

PHYSICS, BIOLOGY, PROPERTIES OF FIBERS, WOOL, SIMPLE MACHINE

HOW LONG IT TAKES

20 to 30 minutes to learn to spin, longer to spin all your wool

WHAT YOU NEED

scissors
string
a drop spindle
wool roving and/or the rolags from the dog hair carding project (p. 64)

Once you've carded your wool into a rolag, give this one a spin. You'll experience the physics of textiles as you train wool fibers into a strong thread that you can use to knit.

ROVING
is rolag that has been pulled into a loose strand that is ready for spinning.

"It helped me to do it slowly at first."
—Daniela, on learning to spin

WHAT TO DO

1 CUT AN 18-INCH PIECE of string and tie it to the stick of the spindle, right near the wheel. Thread the other end of the string through the hook on the stick.

2 STRETCH OUT a length of roving about 24 inches long. Pull it thinner and harder than you might think possible. You might pull it apart at first. If this happens try again until you feel more confident of how far you can pull it without tearing it apart. It helps to hold your hands 4 to 6 inches apart as you stretch it out.

3 WIND THE ROVING around the string, twisting them together and threading both through the hook.

4 THIS IS THE TRICKY PART, where you'll feel like you need three hands: (1) one to hold the thread and wool fibers about 12 inches above the hook, (2) one to pull the fibers into the spinning thread, and (3) one to set the spindle spinning.

5 DON'T GET FRUSTRATED. Keep trying until you get the hang of it. Let the spindle spin down between your knees so you can use your knees to grab it and stop it to stay in control.

6 WIND YOUR THREAD into a ball to make it ready for knitting.

> **WHAT TO EXPECT** A bit of wool threaded through the hook is pulled down and spun into a thread as the spindle revolves.
>
> At first your yarn will be lumpy. Keep trying. You'll get the hang of letting the spin and downward pull create tension and twist, and gradually add more roving to it.

> **WHAT'S GOING ON** Fibers that are twisted in a continuous direction in spinning will hold together to make a thread.

DROP SPINDLE is a tool for spinning wool fibers (also called roving) into yarn. It's a stick with a hook on one end and a wheel on the other. The wheel doesn't revolve around the stick—instead, the whole spindle revolves together as it hangs loose.

"I'm spinning at the bottom and pulling up from the top. The tension of the twist pulls the wool into a thread."
—Desiree

INSIDER INFO: Textile artist Doug Dickinson taught us to hold up the thread (hand 1), quickly set the spindle spinning (3); and then lift the spindle hand to pull new roving into the thread (2). He showed us how to drape the wool fiber behind us over one shoulder, so that we could feed it into hand 1.

FINGER KNITTING

Use this basic process to create an interlocking mesh—and a collar for your dog!

SAFETY CHECK

TRICKY	WHO YOU NEED

	JUST YOU

SUPERVISION: SCISSORS

CONCEPTS

TEXTILE STRUCTURE, CONSTRUCTION PROCESS, TENSION

HOW LONG IT TAKES

30 to 60 minutes to make a long enough strand for a dog collar

WHAT YOU NEED

yarn
scissors

Textiles—including interlocking textiles—are used in medicine, science, and engineering as well as clothing. Understanding them can shed light on how skin, scales, bark, leaves, and other natural materials are constructed.

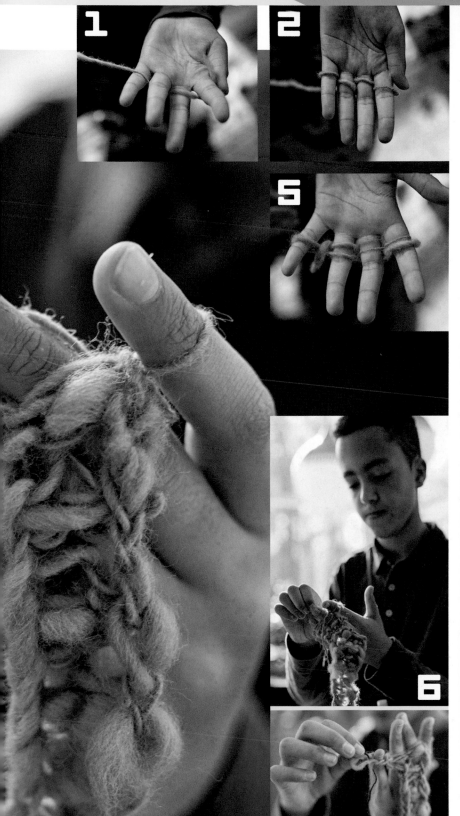

1 TIE THE END of a ball of yarn around the index finger of your nondominant hand.

2 KEEP YOUR nondominant hand palm up. Using your dominant hand, weave the yarn in and out your fingers three times, until each of your fingers has two strands across. To be specific: below your middle finger, above your ring finger, below your pinky and then back the other way, above the pinky, below the ring finger, above the middle finger, below the index finger, then back again, above the index finger, below the middle finger, above the ring finger, below the pinky.

3 NOW, SET THE YARN down a minute. For each finger, pick up the bottom piece of yarn and pull it toward you. Lift it over the top piece of yarn. It will be a loop; place the loop over the finger. Go on to the other three fingers and do the same thing.

4 GO BACK to weaving the yarn in and out your fingers. Each time you have two strings on a finger, loop the bottom one up over the finger.

5 CONTINUE WEAVING and looping, weaving and looping. The loops will begin to form a clump behind your hand, and eventually the clump will form a tube down your hand. Keep going until you think the tube is long enough to go around your dog's neck. End with the index finger.

6 NOW BIND OFF: Take the loop from the index finger and put it on the middle finger. Then lift the middle finger loop up over the index finger string. Now move the middle finger string to the ring finger. Loop the ring finger string up over the middle finger string. Now move the ring finger string to the pinky. Loop the pinky string up over the ring finger string.

Continued on next page

8

! **7 CUT OFF** the yarn with 12 inches to spare. Loop the tail through the pinky loop and take it off the pinky. Pull the yarn tight to knot it. (Check with a grown-up about how long it should be, so the collar's not too tight.)

8 PUT THE COLLAR around the dog's neck and use the loose end of the yarn to connect to the other end of the tube and complete the ring.

> WHAT TO EXPECT Your finger knitting will create a cylinder made of interlocking stitches—the loops from your fingers.

> WHAT'S GOING ON You're creating a mesh—interlocking loops that are all connected together with similar amounts of "tension"—meaning that they're of a roughly uniform size and shape. This creates a fabric with strength, flexibility, and "give." Think of a chain-link fence, chain mail armor, fishing net, or even T-shirt material. They all have the same basic composition. Try knitting with knitting needles to compare a plane of mesh with a cylinder.

INFRARED INTERFERENCE

Experiment with the infrared signal of a remote control.

CONCEPTS
LIGHT, PHYSICS, ENGINEERING

> ### HOW LONG IT TAKES
> 20 to 30 minutes

> ### WHAT YOU NEED
> remote control (possibly several of different types)
> various materials to experiment with, including wood, fabric, stone, paper, foil, china, stoneware, etc.
> OPTIONAL: mirrors, digital camera or smartphone camera

Here's a technological phenomenon that literally takes place in front of you all the time. Take a closer look at the workings of your TV remote control (or any remote control) to analyze and affect the system involved.

ANIMAL SUPERPOWERS

WHAT TO DO

1 START BY LOOKING at the top of a remote control to see if you can see the infrared light signal. You shouldn't be able to see it with your naked eye, but you may be able to see it through the lens of a camera because of the filters that allow you to view it. Not all remote controls worked for this. Remotes with signals visible through cameras tended not to have buttons that lit when used.

2 ESTABLISH that your remote can be used to power your TV, radio, or other device, or to control volume, channels, etc.

3 NEXT, SEE whether you can block the remote signal with different materials.

2

BONUS

Aim the remote away from the TV or radio. Does it work? Can you use a mirror to reflect the signal back at the TV? What about two mirrors?

3

"If you wrap the remote in aluminum foil, it doesn't work!"
—Justice

WHAT TO EXPECT Various materials will allow the infrared signal to pass through them.

WHAT'S GOING ON A television remote control uses a code of signals of infrared light waves to communicate with the television. Each command has a different signal, invisible to the human eye (but visible to certain cameras, as well as to certain animals, especially snakes, that use the light to locate prey). The light passes through or around many different materials. You can prove the existence of this invisible ray of light by seeing how it commands the TV and by showing how it behaves around your test materials.

"We tried it from outside and it worked."
—Kamari

OUR TRY

Our remote's signal went through most of the materials we tried—so many that we thought somehow that it was hooked into the house's wireless Internet and that it didn't matter which way we fired its signal, it was still reaching the TV! But no—we were able to stop the signal with several different objects. Here are some of our results:

- Plexiglass: yes, the remote still works
- paper: yes
- foil: yes
- bubble wrap: yes
- plastic wrap: yes
- velvet: yes
- wrapped velvet: yes
- upholstery fabric: yes
- A chinaware pot finally blocked it, as did a Belgian block stone we brought in from outside.

Justice tried to see if it went through the mirror. It didn't. But the mirror would not bounce the signal back either, so that was strange.

QUESTION THIS!

How far can an infrared signal travel? Does it have to travel through space uninterrupted to communicate with the TV? What's the greatest distance from which it will work?

BLUBBER GLOVES

Who's got blubber? A whale, a walrus, and you!

SAFETY CHECK

SIMPLE

WHO YOU NEED

GRAB A GROWN-UP & FRIEND

SUPERVISION: ICE, PLASTIC BAGS

CONCEPTS

BIOLOGY, ZOOLOGY, PHYSICS, INSULATION CAPABILITIES OF VARIOUS MATERIALS

HOW LONG IT TAKES
30 minutes

WHAT YOU NEED
large Ziploc bags (we used 1-quart bags, but you might want bigger ones for bigger hands or to experiment with more insulating materials)
insulating materials:
- shortening (the solid white kind in the can, not the liquid oil)
- Styrofoam packing peanuts or broken up Styrofoam cups
- cotton balls, feathers, or other natural materials

duct tape
nitrile gloves (like a doctor or dentist uses)
bucket of ice and water

Extremely cold climates are chock-full of life. What kind of adaptations do polar animals have to allow them to thrive in these environments? Learn about one survival tool here.

1-3

"The side of my hand isn't cold but the bottom is. The Styrofoam got pushed aside. With the Styrofoam all around my hand [after the boys adjusted it for her] the Styrofoam is better than the blubber. A teeny tiny bit of cold is sneaking in. I guess that's why Styrofoam works for coffee cups."
—Kamari

QUESTION THIS!

How does it feel? This is a subjective experiment—meaning that the subject's impressions and feelings as she compares her two hands will provide your data about the insulating properties of different materials.

WHAT TO DO

1 ASSEMBLE A BLUBBER GLOVE using shortening. Fill a Ziploc bag three-quarters full.

2 HAVE THE SUBJECT put on nitrile gloves. (She can be tested without gloves if she's willing.)

3 INSERT the subject's hands in Ziploc bags—one empty and one with shortening. Zip and tape the bags closed.

4 HAVE THE SUBJECT place her hands in the icy water for as long as she can stand.

5 ASK WHICH HAND stays warmer.

6 REPEAT with different insulating materials. Compare.

BONUS

Kamari wanted to know what would happen to shortening if it was frozen. Find out yourself!

WHAT TO EXPECT Some of the materials placed in the bag around the subject's hand will prevent cold from reaching her hand better than others.

WHAT'S GOING ON Fat—even a vegetable-based fat like shortening—insulates animals like you from cold, so it provides a decent substitute for blubber, the layer of fat that seals, whales, walrus, polar bears, and other marine animals in polar climates have under their skin.

Other materials, such as Styrofoam, keep drinks warm because they don't conduct heat, so it doesn't escape through the sides and bottom of the cup. (For more on Styrofoam, see That Sinking Feeling, p. 48.)

By the way, a bucket full of ice to which you add water is a fair representation of the temperature and texture of the water around ice floes—where animals such as seals and whales tend to live.

OUR TRY

Oops—to make a better comparison between insulated and noninsulated hands, we should have had Kamari place her hand in the water wearing only a Ziploc bag on top of her nitrile glove. That way the only variable for her hands would be the so-called blubber layer. Other materials we would have liked to try included fur, feathers, and Mylar.

SPECIAL F/X

BAM! That's what we found ourselves saying a lot while trying out these projects. For some, it was a sound effect. For others, it was a shout of surprise. For all, it let us express what we felt when we got to the moment when—well, try it yourself. You'll see!

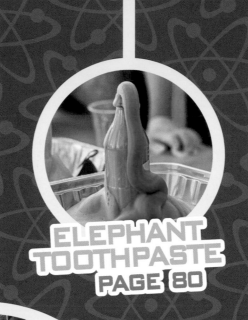

ELEPHANT TOOTHPASTE
PAGE 80

DRY ICE BUBBLE
PAGE 84

PAPER ENGINEERING
PAGE 78

COLOR EXPLOSION
PAGE 82

INSTANT SLUSH
PAGE 86

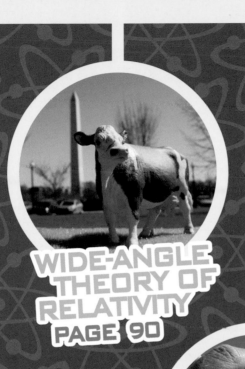

WIDE-ANGLE THEORY OF RELATIVITY
PAGE 90

BATTERY COIL TRAIN
PAGE 94

A WEIRD PERSPECTIVE
PAGE 92

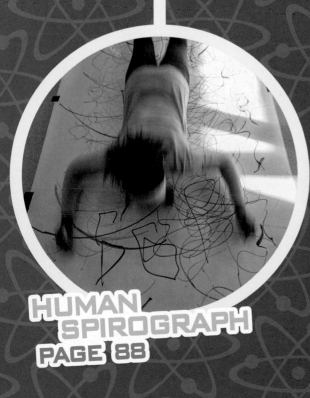

HUMAN SPIROGRAPH
PAGE 88

BOTTLE OF STRING
PAGE 96

PAPER ENGINEERING

Guess what's going to pop up?

HOW LONG IT TAKES
One hour, including drawing time

WHAT YOU NEED
9 flat paper bags, all the same size, not exceeding 9 inches
markers, paint, or crayons
glue stick
scissors
OPTIONAL: masking tape, hole punch, string

Origami practices apply not just to making paper animals (or airplanes) but to engineering efforts for remotely operated pop-up robots involved in espionage.

INSIDE INFO
One of the most ambitious and far-reaching concepts now being explored by the U.S. Department of Defense and other agencies developing new methods in espionage is the micro-aerial vehicle, or MAV—die-cut remote-control robots that fold flat, pop up, and can be assembled. Some of the flying MAVs resemble birds and insects so closely that they can hang out in plain sight, doing surveillance with minimal potential for detection. This activity lets you discover the kind of engineering involved in designing pop-ups—or party decorations!

WHAT TO DO

1 COLOR THE BAGS on both sides. Use any kind of design you choose. You can also opt for bags that come striped or in different colors.

2 LAY ONE BAG on the table in front of you so that the opening is toward you. Your bag should have one side of the opening longer than the other. Place the longer side on the bottom.

3 DRAW A STRIP of glue across the end of the bag that is away from you, then down the center of the bag toward you, so that you draw a big T in glue. Don't get glue on the long side of the bottom.

4 LAY THE NEXT BAG, oriented the same as the first bag, directly on top of the first, evening up the edges.

5 DRAW THE T of glue on the second bag and stick the third on top. Continue until all nine bags are glued together, each on top of the next.

6 TURN THE BAGS so that the openings are away from you. Find the center point of the sides of the bags and the opening. Cut from one side to the center of the opening, then from the other side to the center of the opening.

OPTIONAL: If you want, cut shapes along the folded edges of the bags below the center point, cutting through all bags at once.

STOP! What shape do you think your bags will make when you open or pop them up?

> **WHAT TO EXPECT** Your bags will expand to form a three-dimensional (3-D) star.

> **WHAT'S GOING ON** Through simple geometry, your gluing and cutting shaped a 2-D bag into a 3-D form.

6

"Whoa! It's magic like a Chinese lantern that you could hang up at the festivals!"
—Mychal-Jael

QUESTION THIS!

What other shapes and structures can you form from flat bags? What about from shaped bags like paper grocery bags? Or from boxes?

INSIDE INFO
To hang your star, punch a hole through one point and thread a string through it.

OUR TRY

When Alex did this, he cut the wrong end of the bag—the closed end instead of the open end. But it turned out *not* to be a glitch ...

> **GLITCH** As a result, Alex didn't make a star—he made a three-dimensional rectangular chain and two pinwheels.

ELEPHANT TOOTHPASTE

Can you replicate an extreme reaction?

SAFETY CHECK

TRICKY

WHO YOU NEED

GRAB A GROWN-UP & FRIEND

SUPERVISION: CHEMICAL REACTIONS

CONCEPTS

CHEMISTRY

HOW LONG IT TAKES
30 minutes

WHAT YOU NEED
For each tube of toothpaste (bottle with a reaction inside):
 16-ounce empty plastic soda or water bottle with narrow neck
 foil cake pan with 2-inch sides
 funnel
 ½ cup 20-volume peroxide, sold in a beauty supply store; needs to be a 6 percent solution (see safety tips, p. 7)
 squirt of dish detergent
 3 drops to a teaspoon of food coloring
 glass measuring cup, beaker, or clear plastic cup
 1 teaspoon of yeast
 2 tablespoons of very warm water
 plastic spoon
SAFETY EQUIPMENT: safety goggles, lab apron, nitrile gloves

Replication is an important part of science. If someone can't copy your procedure and get the same results, your science comes into question. We had seen this reaction demonstrated on television and wanted to try it for ourselves.

OUR TRY

We worked together to decide on the two colors we would mix for each bottle: blue and green, blue and purple, red and yellow. Our non-chemical team (not handling chemicals) made the yeast mixture in a measuring cup. The chemical team (handling chemicals, so protected by goggles, gloves, and aprons) poured the yeast mixture into the bottles, and we all stood back to watch the results. The "toothpaste" spurted out in gorgeous shapes and textures, some of it two-toned, especially the blue/purple mix. It overflowed the "tubes" and flowed into the pans. Then, quickly, the reaction slowed. But the bubbles continued to move inside the tubes even after the initial formation was over, so the ongoing reaction could be observed.

WHAT TO DO

1 STAND soda bottle in foil pan.

2 INSERT FUNNEL in neck of soda bottle.

! 3 ADD ½ cup peroxide, detergent, and food coloring.

4 IN MEASURING CUP, beaker, or plastic cup, combine yeast and warm water. Combine with plastic spoon.

5 POUR YEAST mixture into soda bottle and remove funnel.

! WARNING: *Avoid touching or getting the chemicals on skin or clothing.*

WHAT TO EXPECT A very foamy tube of colored "toothpaste" will emerge from the bottle and overflow for up to half an hour before the reaction slows and stops. You may feel some heat coming off it, too.

WHAT'S GOING ON Hydrogen peroxide normally decomposes (breaks down into separate elements), and combining it with detergent and yeast (a catalyst) speeds up the process. Here's the chemical formula:

$2 H_2O_2$ *turns to* $2 H_2O$ *and* O_2.

As the oxygen emanates from the reaction, it creates bubbles. The detergent speeds up the foaming. The reaction is "exothermic," meaning it produces heat (and steam as well). **WARNING:** *Heat and steam can be dangerous. Be cautious and don't get too close.*

"I feel like I'm holding water, but it's hardening on my fingers. In the bottle it looked so much different than when it came out."
—Samuel

COLOR EXPLOSION

We just had to try this suggestion from one of our scientists, Kameron.

SAFETY CHECK

SIMPLE

WHO YOU NEED

JUST YOU

CONCEPTS

CHEMISTRY

HOW LONG IT TAKES
15 to 20 minutes (including waiting time for reaction to end)

WHAT YOU NEED
shallow baking dish with a flat bottom (Depth should be the same across entire dish; it can be any shape—round and rectangular are interesting and beautiful.)
milk (We used whole milk.)
food coloring
dish detergent

Some experiments just have to be experienced personally! Although we'd seen the instructions for it, we weren't that impressed before. Luckily, Kameron convinced us to give it a shot!

3

"It looks like the soap is pushing away the color. The colors look like tropical birds. So many cool shapes!"
—Audrey

WHAT TO DO

1 FILL THE DISH with about ½ inch of milk.

2 ADD DOTS OF COLORS using food coloring. Make whatever pattern you like, but use plenty of colorful dots.

3 DROP JUST ONE drip of dish detergent in the middle of the milk.

WHAT TO EXPECT The colors will sink in response to the dish detergent, then emerge again, marbleizing, and combining, before stabilizing and standing still.

WHAT'S GOING ON Milk is an emulsion, a suspension of fat droplets in water. This means they're not mixed in, just hanging in the milk. Food coloring sits in drops in the water, too, making a stable system—until the dish detergent is added. Dish detergents are meant to separate out dirt or grease so they can be washed away. When the dish detergent is added, the suspension is broken up, and the fat droplets all rush to combine with each other, causing the blossoming of color.

TWEAKS AND TWISTS Use a small plate full of craft glue instead of milk, and repeat the experiment with the food coloring and dish detergent. Let the glue dry and remove the glue disk from the plate for a visible souvenir of this experiment.

"It's like that experiment I know with water, pepper, and soap. You shake pepper on top of the water and when you put in soap it pushes all the pepper away."
—Cori

QUESTION THIS!

How could you slow down or speed up this reaction?

"I think I have a name for this: Color Explosion!"
—Cori

BONUS

After the colors marbleize, try to transfer the pattern onto a piece of paper. Drop the paper flat onto the milk's surface and allow the liquid to soak it for a moment or two. Then lift the paper by several corners, flip it, and transfer to a paper towel to dry. Then spray it with Clear-Coat or another acrylic art spray to preserve the colors.

DRY ICE BUBBLE

Use frozen carbon dioxide (dry ice) to make an enormous smoking bubble. Fabulous!

SAFETY CHECK

DIFFICULT

WHO YOU NEED

GRAB A GROWN-UP

SUPERVISION: DRY ICE

CONCEPTS

CHEMISTRY, PHYSICS, BUBBLE MEMBRANE, FREEZING

HOW LONG IT TAKES
About 20 minutes

WHAT YOU NEED
large mixing bowl
water
dry ice (see safety tips, p. 7)
dish soap
small bowl
rag—old T-shirt or sock
SAFETY EQUIPMENT: safety goggles, insulated gloves
NOTE ON DRY ICE : Ask at a grocery store about a source for dry ice. Some sell it. We had to go to an ice supplier. You can find those in your phone book Yellow Pages or on the Internet. Don't put dry ice on your counter or floor—it might crack it. And definitely don't let it get on your skin. When you're finished with it, set it in a bucket to melt.

🔍 **DRY ICE** is frozen carbon dioxide. Its temperature is around -100°F. Handle it only with insulated mittens or protective gloves, **never with bare hands.**

There's a knack to this one. Get the knack and you'll blow quite a bubble. You'll blow people's minds, too!

"Superfun experiment."
—Maya

SUBLIMATION: *going straight from solid to vapor without a liquid stage*

3-4

6

WHAT TO DO

1 ADD A CUP of water to the mixing bowl.

! 2 HAVE AN ADULT add a handful of dry ice to the water. It will fog or smoke.

3 POUR DISH SOAP into small bowl.

4 SOAK THE RAG in the dish soap.

5 WRING OUT the rag.

6 DRAW THE RAG across the top of the large mixing bowl, coating the edges and pulling a thin film of soap across the top.

WHAT TO EXPECT As the ultracold dry ice reacts with the water, it warms the air. This rises and pushes the soap film up to make a big cloudy bubble that eventually bursts. The cloud created by the dry ice may seem to spill over the edges of the bowl when the bubble bursts.

WHAT'S GOING ON Dry ice is ultracold. When it hits about -69°F, it vaporizes, skipping liquid form and going straight from being a solid to being a gas. Combining it with water creates water vapor or fog. Its molecules rise and expand, pushing at the light membrane of the bubble until the pressure bursts the bubble. This is sublimation.

OUR TRY

We used the big bubble formula (see p. 18). You might get a stronger bubble—and therefore a higher bubble—with a different formula. Try that! It takes a little practice to drag the rag across the bowl in a manner that allows the membrane to form. Our method was to start under the edge of the bowl closest to us, then push the rag over to the other side and over the far brim. Pulling the rag up before hitting that brim often broke the bubble too soon.

"Give yourself confidence! If someone says he can't do it, say 'Yes, you can!' "
—Antonio

"When the dry ice warms up it makes the air hot and it rises. The fog expands and particles are bouncing around really fast."
—Electra

INSTANT SLUSH

Think soda is supercool? Try this!

SAFETY CHECK

TRICKY

WHO YOU NEED

GRAB A GROWN-UP

CONCEPTS

CHEMISTRY, PHYSICS, BUBBLE MEM-BRANE, FREEZING

HOW LONG IT TAKES
3 to 4 hours, including freezer time

WHAT YOU NEED
2 to 3 16.9- to 20-ounce bottles of soda
freezer
clear glasses
candy thermometer for assessing temperature of freezer
some ice from your freezer

Expose liquids to extreme temperatures inside your freezer. If you time things correctly (through a series of trials), your results will be extreme, too.

SUPERCOOLING
is a process in which a substance is cooled below its freezing point without solidification or crystallization.

WHAT TO DO

1 SHAKE A BOTTLE of room-temperature soda and place it in the freezer. Wait two to three hours. Check it periodically.

2 CHILL A GLASS in the freezer along with the bottle. Remove both at the same time. Open the cap extremely slowly and pour gently into the chilled glass. Instant slush!

3 HAVE A GLASS on hand that is at room temperature. Open your chilled soda bottle and pour it into the glass. Add one small chip of ice. Instant slush!

4 WHAT IF ICE FORMS only at the top of your glass? Stir it and it should form instant slush!

! BONUS

Find out what's really in soda by asking an adult to help you boil it until all the water evaporates (see safety tips, p. 7). What's left in the pan? Some sodas leave a lot of syrup, showing the amount of sugar and chemicals in them.

WHAT TO EXPECT If the liquid is super-cooled, it will only take a bit of agitation (shaking) to get it to slush up and begin to solidify.

WHAT'S GOING ON The part that freezes is the water. The water is supercooled to the extent that it is just waiting for a slight change in conditions to solidify. The syrup—the part of the drink that provides the color and flavor—gets trapped between the ice crystals, making it slushy.

GLITCH The trick of this experiment is finding the right amount of time for your freezer. Some people had success at about 2 hours 15 minutes, and others as long as 3 hours, 5 minutes. Your supercooled soda will still look like liquid when you remove the bottle from the freezer. If it's frozen, you've let it stay in there too long.

TWEAKS AND TWISTS

If it starts freezing too soon and you really want that instant slush, you can always squeeze it out of the bottle.

Canned soda works, too, but it can be hard to open slowly—and hard to squeeze out if it freezes.

Try the same experiment with sports drinks.

Consider the difference between bottles frozen standing vertically or lying down horizontally.

OUR TRY

The first time we tried this, we put several six-packs of soda in the freezer (separate them first) and removed one every 15 minutes to determine what the optimum supercooling time was for our freezer. We got no slushing action in bottles frozen for under 2½ hours. You might try starting by taking a bottle out at that point and then every 5 to 15 minutes after that until you figure out the optimum supercooling time for your freezer. Note: Our freezer was at 20°F.

HUMAN SPIROGRAPH

What happens when you combine a small motion with a large motion—and add drawing to make it all come to life?

INSIDER INFO:
Are you really a human spirograph? A spirograph is a toy with two parts: a large piece (usually with a geometric shape like a circle or triangle) with teeth like a gear; it forms the path over which the smaller piece travels. The smaller piece has a hole for a pen point. The pattern it follows changes depending on the path dictated by the larger piece.

SAFETY CHECK

TRICKY

WHO YOU NEED

GRAB A FRIEND

CONCEPTS

PHYSICS, MOTION, PHYSIOLOGY, MECHANICS, ART

HOW LONG IT TAKES
30 minutes

WHAT YOU NEED
large uncarpeted room or hall
huge rolls of paper
masking tape
skateboard and/or exercise ball
big markers

This experiment is beautiful in its simplicity, and simple in its beauty. To try it is to fall in love with art, with math, with motion. See if we're exaggerating!

WHAT TO DO

The idea here is that you get the motion of the body going in a continuous pattern—in other words, back and forth on the skateboard or the exercise ball while lying on your stomach, with the assistance of another person.

1 TAPE A BIG SHEET of paper to the floor.

2 POSITION THE SKATEBOARD at one edge of the paper.

3 LIE ON the skateboard on your stomach.

4 HAVE YOUR PARTNER hold you by your feet.

5 FIRST, PRACTICE. Have your partner push you by the feet, forward across the paper, then pull you back to the edge. Practice until you get comfortable with a steady back and forth motion.

6 NOW DO THE SAME skateboard-pushing while holding colored markers in your hands, one color in each hand. Plan a small motion to make with your hands, and do it at the edge of the paper while the skateboard is still. For example, you might make a circle, a letter *B* or *S*, a zigzag forward, or a big sideways swoop like a seagull. Do the same pattern with both hands.

7 NOW KEEP that hand motion continuous while your partner pushes you back and forth on the skateboard.

8 SEE HOW your hand motion pattern and the pattern made as your partner pushes and pulls you forward and backward affects the pattern on the paper.

WHAT TO EXPECT The repetition of your hand motion as you're pushed across the paper in a full-body motion will be regular, continual, and unexpected!

WHAT'S GOING ON Well, how would you describe it? Small motion or pattern + additional motion or pattern = a third motion or pattern.

"It looks like a hot dog .... This is art! It should be in the Museum of Modern Art. This is interesting. It looks like DNA." —Sayla

"You could see the initial patterns but when you start moving it's a whole different pattern." —Henry

QUESTION THIS!

How else could you change the patterns in your drawings?

OUR TRY

We did this in the lobby of the National Geographic Building in Washington, D.C., using one of Matt's backdrop papers. Henry started with circles, which made a lovely scrolling pattern as Samuel pushed him back and forth on the skateboard. Arya tried making squares, Sayla made zigzags and mustaches. They all tried different patterns, then tried the exercise balls. It was hard to maintain any shape while doing so.

BONUS

Now that you've seen what happens when you go straight forward and back on the skateboard, repeat the experiment while lying face-down on a big exercise ball. This time, your partner holds you by the shoulders, back, or hips and pushes you along a curved path while you attempt to draw your small pattern. What happens?

WIDE-ANGLE
THEORY OF
RELATIVITY

Our photographer, Matt, shows us tricks of the trade.

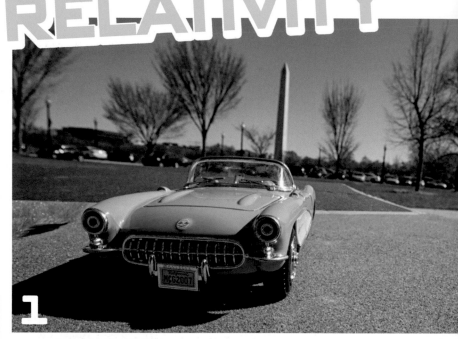

1

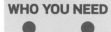

CONCEPTS

OPTICS, VISUAL PERCEPTION, PERSPECTIVE, GEOMETRY, PHOTOGRAPHY

HOW LONG IT TAKES
One hour

WHAT YOU NEED
model cars, toy animals, and/or action figures
sheet of cardboard or foam core with artificial pavement, snow, or grass (We got ours at a hobby/model train shop.)
an area with people, buildings, cars
camera
(Hint: Read through the activity first to get an idea of what you want to do and what you will need to do it.)

Our gang was awestruck when they grasped the trick to photographic effects involving perception and angles. Thanks to Matt, they'll never see miniature cars and cows in the same way!

1a

1c

1d

Here's how to do the examples that Matt showed us. From this you can get creative, extrapolating (extending) his methods to ideas of your own.

1 PARKING CARS TRICK:

Make a model car seem to be the same size as full-size cars.

- **a** For this, Matt used a model car and a sheet of cardboard onto which he had fastened model-shop pavement.

- **b** He looked for a background of cars in a parking lot. The parking lot had some empty spaces.

- **c** Holding up the model car, Matt walked toward and away from the parking lot until he figured out exactly how far he needed to be in order for the model car to appear to be the same size as the full-size cars in the parking lot.

- **d** Matt set the model car on the model pavement and placed his setup so that, through his camera lens, the model car seemed to fit right into the space in the parking lot.

2 GRAZING COWS: Make the Washington Monument look as if it has cows grazing around it, as it once did.

- **a** Matt set up toy cows on cardboard with fake grass on it.

- **b** He placed the grass so that it seemed to be just a hill in front of the grass (in the background) at the foot of the Washington Monument.

- **c** He adjusted the distance of the cows to the monument until the cows seemed to be full-sized compared to the monument.

WHAT'S GOING ON How do science-fiction moviemakers use this trick to make model spaceships and the like look full-size?

Henry: "I see it in the viewfinder and it looks so fine until you see the cardboard is in the picture."

Samuel: "Maybe you should move the car closer toward the cow."

Matt: "Do you see how getting low works? For something like this to look bigger, you need to get down low. Get right down to the edge at eye level or below."

Arya: "That's really cool! And that's what they did in the Harry Potter movies with Hagrid to make him seem bigger? Our childhood is ruined!"

Samuel: "Going low, low, low. CLICK That looks really cool with the monument sticking up ... whew! CLICK ... I was at the same height, just did different zooms. Now put the big cow in the back and the little cow in the front like it's driving away. CLICK."

"Get the camera! Give it a whirl!"
—Matt

A WEIRD PERSPECTIVE

Your camera is a tool for more tricks of the eye.

SAFETY CHECK

TRICKY

WHO YOU NEED

GRAB SOME FRIENDS

CONCEPTS

Optics, visual perception, perspective, geometry, photography

HOW LONG IT TAKES
One hour

WHAT YOU NEED
an open area
a distant object such as a building, a tree, the moon
camera

Catch the moon in your hands, toss your friend up in the air. Your only limit in this experiment is your imagination.

WHAT TO DO

1 OBJECTIVE: Make someone in the foreground seem to be much larger than an object or person in the background.

- **a** Matt showed us how to make the Washington Monument seem to be standing in the palm of our hands. It takes two people: a person in the foreground pretending to hold the monument, and the second (the photographer) letting the first person know when she's got the forced perspective precisely right—and the monument squarely in her palm.

- **b** If you position a person correctly, relative to a distant natural object like the moon, you can make him seem to be holding it, too.

- **c** We experimented with putting a person (or two) in the distant background and positioning a person in the foreground so that it looks as if she can pick the others up in her fingers, have them lean against her palm, and so on.

> **CONSIDER THIS** We worked hard to create images that really trick the eye. What is the effect of the ones that fail through misusing scale (relative size) and angles? Is there a way to use these accidental effects to tell a different story?

> **WHAT'S GOING ON** This demonstration makes use of visual point of view and perspective, phenomena of scale (relative size), and angles, which artists must learn in order to make objects appear to be at a distance. Once you know these methods, you can use them to trick the eye into "thinking" that very unrealistic relationships exist!

BATTERY COIL TRAIN

Create an electromagnetic field to make a floating train.

SAFETY CHECK

DIFFICULT

WHO YOU NEED

GRAB A GROWN-UP

SUPERVISION: WIRE CUTTERS, PLIERS, ELECTRICITY, HEAT

CONCEPTS

ENGINEERING, ELECTROMAGNETICS

HOW LONG IT TAKES
45 minutes

WHAT YOU NEED
6-yard spool of 20-gauge, uninsulated copper wire (bought at a craft store)
wire cutters
small pliers
1 wooden dowel, ¾-inch diameter, about 18 inches long
6 neodymium magnets ½ x ⅛ inch (Disc N48), available online or at an electronics store
AAA batteries (see safety tips, p. 7)
SAFETY EQUIPMENT: Gloves
OPTIONAL: Scotch tape

Tricky, tricky! But get it right and you'll feel the force—a combination of forces, actually, strong enough to drive a train.

"The coil can't have curves on it or it won't conduct electricity. The curve pulls the spirals apart."
—Samuel

1

3-4

INSIDER INFO:
Arya managed this task ingeniously. She attached the first stack of magnets to the battery and then placed the second stack on the back of her hand. The magnets are so strong that they attracted right through her hand, showing her which side attracted without getting stuck on.

"It's a one-time train! The battery and coil get hot and wear out if you leave it all connected."
—Henry

5

"I feel like I'm watching a snake digesting its food."
—Sayla (watching the battery travel through the coil)

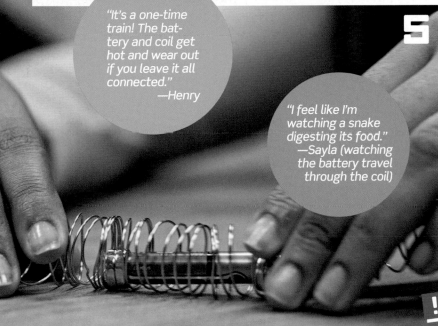

GLITCH The battery repels the coil and pops out of it? Turn it around so it attracts and insert it again. If the battery "train" doesn't move at all, check the orientation of your magnets.

Kinks and spaces in your coil can mess up the electromagnetic flow so that the solenoid coil works no better than the spiral on your notebook. Use the dowel and pliers to form the tightest, smoothest coil you can.

Finally, the battery can get hot and burn out its energy quickly if left to flounder in place inside a loose coil. Our group agreed, this one is not for the fainthearted! It takes patience and precision.

WHAT TO DO

1 CAREFULLY OPEN the copper wire and begin to wrap it tightly around the dowel to form a coil with each wound loop right up against the last. Unrolling packaged wires too quickly can cause kinks. It's better to slowly unroll the wire as you wind it around the dowel, using the pliers, to form the coil. When the coil is finished, remove the dowel.

2 SEPARATE THE MAGNETS into two stacks of three and do your best to keep them apart.

3 PICK UP A STACK of three magnets and attach them to one end of a AAA battery.

4 NOW TAKE the other stack of three magnets. Your job here is a tricky one: figure out which side of the magnets is attracted to the magnets already on the battery. Do your best not to allow them to stick on to those magnets! (See Insider Info.) Once you have figured out which side wants to attract, move these magnets to the other end of the battery and attach them with the attracting side toward the battery and the repelling side away from it.

5 PLACE THE BATTERY inside the copper coil.

! WARNING: *Any time you are conducting electricity it can be hot. Be careful. If needed, wear gloves. This experiment did result in some heat.*

BONUS

Try using Scotch tape to link two or more solenoids to make a longer track. Note that you have to have the magnetism working in the same direction for both solenoids or the "train" will not pass through. If this happens, try turning the coil the other way.

> WHAT TO EXPECT The battery will move through the coil by an unseen force!

> WHAT'S GOING ON The copper is wound into a solenoid, a coil, spiral, or helix shape that conducts electrical current in a constant, steady, magnetic flow capable of pulling the battery through it.

BOTTLE OF STRING

Here are a few methods for making plastic bottles into string.

SAFETY CHECK

TRICKY

WHO YOU NEED

GRAB A GROWN-UP

SUPERVISION: PENCIL SHARPENER BLADE, SCISSORS, KNIFE

CONCEPTS

RECYCLING, ENGINEERING, PLASTICS, MECHANICS

HOW LONG IT TAKES

One hour

WHAT YOU NEED

mechanical (not electric) pencil sharpener with screw-on blades
wooden board
ruler
2 small wood screws
screwdriver
6 washers
scissors or craft knife
plastic bottles

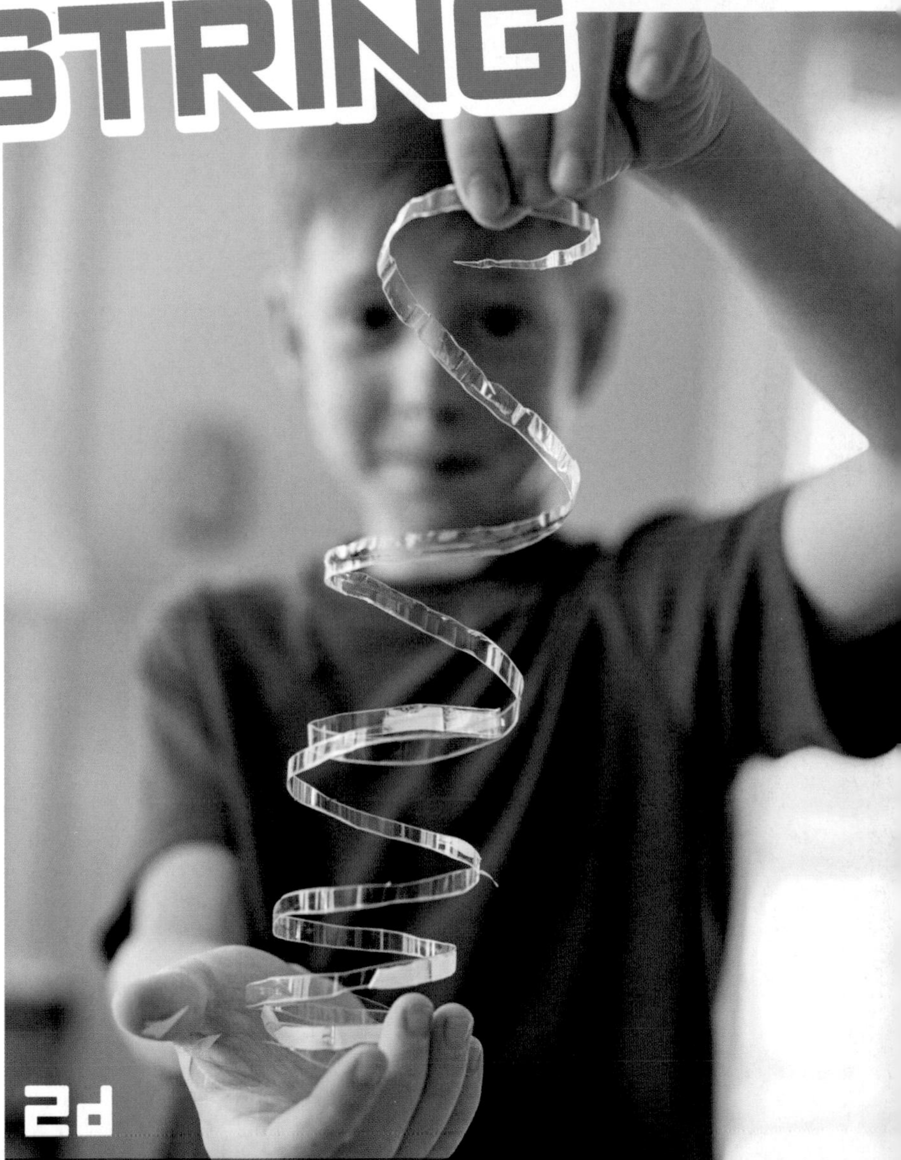

2d

This project requires you to work the angles, make the cut, and use your pull. Connect them all just right and you'll have the world by a string.

WHAT TO DO

1 MAKE A STRING-CUTTING MACHINE.

METHOD 1:

- **a** Unscrew a pencil sharpener blade from the sharpener.

- **b** Measure the length of the blade. Measure the same distance apart on a board and mark it. This is where you will place your screws.

- **c** Place three washers on each screw and attach the screws on the board. Do not screw them in tightly.

- **d** Have an adult supervise as you carefully place the sharpener blade, blade side down, between the top and middle washer in both screws. Screw the screws on firmly (see photo 2c).

2 CUT STRING.

- **a** Use a craft knife or scissors to cut the bottom off a plastic bottle.

- **b** Along the edge of the bottle, start making the bottle string with a small cut.

- **c** Place the blade of your machine along the cut and begin to cut the string, about ⅛ to ¼ inch wide. Pull the end through under the blade (or just cut with scissors, as Sam did).

- **d** Continue cutting and pulling until you have a long string—one continuous string from one whole bottle is the goal.

> **GLITCH** The Internet is full of ideas and videos for making plastic string, but we were not able to replicate any of them with repeated success. Initially, we had success using a pencil sharpener with one blade removed, flipped, and screwed on at an angle, but when Renuka tried this, the blades kept breaking after cutting a few little strings. We're including this activity because we had the most success, but none of us could create a machine that easily gave us one long, continuous string.

"Do we have to use the pencil sharpener? If the whole point is to see how strong the string is, I'm just using scissors."
—Sam

QUESTION THIS!

How does doubling, folding, and twisting the string affect its strength?

OUR TRY

Our three scientists took different approaches to this challenge.

Alex worked on adapting the pencil sharpener blade to the board structure, flipping the blade. He got it to cut but could not find the right angle and force to get a long string. His string kept cutting off short into chunks.

Renuka tried to get the sharpener blade on the sharpener to work continually. It worked but the positioning of the blade tended to break the blade, and she broke a bunch before giving up.

WATER WAY TO ACT

We would have swum the deepest river or crossed the widest ocean to bring you these water experiments. And you wouldn't think we were drippy to do it. In fact, we're sure you're going to feel a wave of excitement over every one of them.

HYDROPHOBIC GLASS GRAPHICS
PAGE 102

MYO LASER POINTER
PAGE 100

HYDROPHOBIC CLOTHES
PAGE 104

RAINY DAY
SURPRISE
PAGE 107

SCAREDY
SAND
PAGE 112

HERO'S
ENGINE
PAGE 109

BOTTLE WON'T
POUR
PAGE 114

MYO LASER POINTER

In which we make a few points about deep-sea research.

CONCEPTS

WATER PRESSURE, FIBER OPTICS, PHYSICS

HOW LONG IT TAKES
20 to 30 minutes

WHAT YOU NEED
candle, matches (see safety tips, p. 7)
big needle or pins
two 2-liter soda bottles full of water
flashlight
dark or dim area where water spraying around won't matter (We used a shower stall but you can do this outside.)
OPTIONAL: laser pointer, food coloring
SAFETY NOTE: Never look into the light coming from a laser pointer!

In fiber optics, light travels through glass that reflects as if it were water. You can demonstrate these principles with a stream of water.

3-4

WHAT TO DO

1 HAVE AN ADULT HELP you heat a pin or needle and use it to make three holes in one soda bottle full of water. Make each hole at a different level on the bottle: top, middle, and bottom. How does water flow through the different holes?

2 USE A HEATED PIN or needle to make one hole in the second bottle. Place the hole where you think it will create the strongest stream of water. Hold a finger over the hole to stop the water from coming out.

3 AIM A FLASHLIGHT through the soda bottle opposite the hole.

4 MOVE YOUR FINGER. As water streams out, position the flashlight so it lights up the water even as it arcs down, away from the straight path of the light.

> **WHAT TO EXPECT** Even in the dark, the stream of water will be lit up if you have the light positioned correctly. The water will carry the beam of light.

> **WHAT'S GOING ON** Fiber optic cables feature hair-thin strands of glass. Light bounces along the walls of these strands to transmit coded light signals through the length of the cable. This makes fiber optics a fast technology for carrying digital messages from cameras and other sensors sent between tethered submarines on the ocean floor and ships on the surface. A light beam typically travels in a straight line. By using optical cables, light can be transmitted through curves. The water streaming from the bottle demonstrates this principle, as light follows the arcing water, rather than continuing on a straight path. By varying the way you aim the light, you can see the normal straight path, and then direct the light through the water "cable."

> **GLITCH** Keeping the water flowing strongly was difficult for us. We found it necessary to experiment with the bottle cap and the amount of pressure we put on the bottle as we held it. It was easy enough to keep refilling the bottle for repeat tries.

OUR PREDICTION

Kameron: "The lowest stream will be the strongest because it would have the most water coming down to it."

Kamari: "The lowest stream will be the weakest."

Justice: "The middle one will not do anything."

Who do you think was right?

"Opening the lid releases air and allows the water to flow. You have to apply force to the top to get it to flow."
—Justice

INSIDER INFO:
We tried a green laser pointer and flashlights with red, white, and blue filters. Photographer Matt said that blue light carries the farthest (blue light has the largest attenuation, meaning that it is absorbed least in the atmosphere—while in water violet light goes farthest); however, the green laser pointer had stronger, more focused light, so it worked the best in the dimly lit room where we tried this.

QUESTION THIS!

Why does a laser work better than a regular flashlight? Why do different colors of light travel differently?

HYDROPHOBIC GLASS GRAPHICS

"The texture is weird. It's very hard where the spray is. Where the tape was, it's just regular glass. In the sprayed place, the water beaded up. In the unsprayed place, it didn't!"
—Justice

Compare chemicals and create an invisible design—then reveal it.

SAFETY CHECK

TRICKY

WHO YOU NEED

GRAB A GROWN-UP

SUPERVISION: SPRAYING HYDRO-PHOBIC CHEMICALS, GLASS

CONCEPTS

CHEMISTRY, BEHAVIOR OF WATER, ART

HOW LONG IT TAKES
2 to 3 hours

WHAT YOU NEED
hydrophobic spray (see note on p. 103 and safety tips, p. 7)
picture frames with glass
masking tape, stencils, stickers, or other materials that can be stuck onto the glass to prevent spray from reaching it, then removed
watering can
OPTIONAL: craft knife, scissors, Scotch tape, food coloring, natural objects in interesting shapes
SAFETY EQUIPMENT: safety goggles, face mask, lab apron

Experiment with inventions that allow you to control the path of water, and create your own art-work at the same time.

NOTE ABOUT HYDROPHOBIC SPRAYS
Hydrophobic spray is a substance that repels water. It can be found at your local hardware store. Usually it is used to protect surfaces such as wood or concrete from water damage. Compare commercial and homemade hydrophobic chemicals, or just create a design using one or another. Here are two methods to try:

METHOD A:
Commercial hydrophobic spray comes as two cans that are sprayed one after the other.
Spraying: Follow the directions included with the kit for spraying with two cans.

METHOD B:
Homemade hydrophobic spray involves two cans sprayed one after another: Clear-Coat spray and antiperspirant spray.
Spraying: Spray a coat of the clear spray over your design. While it's still wet, spray a coat of antiperspirant over your design. Finish with a second coat of the clear spray.

1

2

5

WHAT TO DO

1 PLAN AND EXECUTE your design on the glass of a picture frame. Use tape, stencils, stickers, natural objects, whatever you want to create your image or message.

2 SPRAY YOUR DESIGN with hydrophobic spray. Don't forget your safety goggles, face mask, and apron. Work in a well-ventilated area that isn't windy.

3 LET YOUR DESIGN DRY for at least an hour.

4 REMOVE the tape, stickers, etc.

5 POUR WATER over the glass.

WHAT TO EXPECT The spray will cover the area around the design, repelling water so that it streams into the design (the masked spaces).

WHAT'S GOING ON The first spray of either the commercial or the homemade process provides a coat of acrylic (plastic) to seal the area. The second spray blocks water from adhering to a surface. In the antiperspirant, the compound cyclopentasiloxane is the component of antiperspirant that functions as the hydrophobic element of this project. This is what keeps your armpits (and clothes) dry when you sweat. Note that deodorant doesn't repel fluid; it just masks the smell of sweat.

GLITCH When Kamari used the commercial spray, it left a whitish film around her design that ruined the possibility of an invisible design. We think maybe we sprayed too close to the glass—that if we held the can at a greater distance, the spray would have been finer, or less concentrated.

QUESTION THIS!

We debated, What's hydrophobic (afraid of water)? Is it the water-resistant place where we sprayed or the spray itself? Or is it the water that's afraid of the spray?

HYDROPHOBIC CLOTHES

Will what you wear get wet?

HOW LONG IT TAKES

2 days: 20 minutes one day to prepare the clothes, 24 hours to allow them to dry, 20 minutes to test them with liquids

WHAT YOU NEED

hydrophobic spray (See note on p. 103 and safety tips, p. 7)
one set of white clothing per person (We shopped for white pants at a secondhand store and found $2 white T-shirts at a craft store.)
clothesline
clothespins
staining liquids that are nontoxic, such as (our choices): tomato juice, cran-raspberry juice, grape juice, chocolate sauce, yellow mustard
paper or plastic cups for the staining liquids
SAFETY EQUIPMENT: safety goggles, lab aprons, face mask

This stuff stains—unless your clothes are protected by hydrophobic coating that really works. Compare and contrast commercial and homemade sprays.

"It's on my foot! It's sliding off the rest of me."
—Sofia

"The tomato juice is sitting right on the surface. It smells like spaghetti ... just take the hit!"
—Emily

WHAT TO DO

1 PLAN YOUR EXPERIMENT.
How many sets of clothing will you compare? How many people do you need? How will you treat each set of clothing? Where will you spray the clothes? Where will you do the demonstration involving pouring staining liquids? (Outside is best.)

2 SPREAD YOUR CLOTHES
on the ground or hang them on a clothes-line. Wear safety equipment while spraying them. (Follow directions; see note above.) Spray the front side only.

3 LET YOUR CLOTHES air dry for at least 24 hours. Don't throw them in a dryer. (Why not? Because spray on one set of wet clothes may get on the other clothes and mess up your experiment. And because you might not want the spray getting on the inside of your dryer.)

Continued on next page

WATER WAY TO ACT

4 HAVE EACH SCIENTIST put on a set of clothes. You can spice things up by not telling the scientists which clothes they're wearing, but keep notes for your own purposes so you can compare how the different treatments vary—and tell them what they were wearing after the demonstration is over. Have them wear safety goggles to avoid liquids splashing in their eyes.

5 PLAN YOUR DEMONSTRATION. Pour staining liquids into cups to ensure that each scientist gets the same amount of each liquid.

6 DUMP THE LIQUIDS down the front of each scientist's clothes. Make a note of what happens. Ask the scientists to predict which treatment was used for their clothes.

WHAT TO EXPECT Clothes that have been treated differently will absorb or repel liquid differently.

WHAT'S GOING ON Hydrophobic sprays coat the fibers in the fabrics of the clothes. Liquid that is poured on them beads up and rolls away, falling off the clothes in the areas that have the most spray.

"I'm excited about this job." —Jamai, the dumper

"Oh! Chocolate syrup next. Open your mouth." —Jameer, a scientist

OUR TRY

We labeled each of four sets of white clothes a, b, c, and d. Then we kept a (secret) notebook saying what each had been sprayed with. Two (a and b) were sprayed with commercial spray, one (c) with homemade spray, one (d) with nothing. We didn't have a clothesline where we were shooting, so we laid our clothes on the ground to spray them, and weighed them down with rocks as they dried. Karisa wore a, Emily wore b, Jameer wore c, and Sofia wore d. Jamai was the dumper.

Karisa and Emily got the least stained. Stuff dripped off them.

Jameer got wetter and more stained. Sofia got it the worst; she was soaked with everything!

RAINY DAY SURPRISE

This one will have you hoping for rain.

SAFETY CHECK

TRICKY

WHO YOU NEED

GRAB A GROWN-UP

SUPERVISION: SPRAYING CHEMICALS

CONCEPTS

WATER BEHAVIOR, LIQUIDS, DESIGN, PUBLIC ART

> ### HOW LONG IT TAKES
> 3 or 4 hours, including an hour to make your design and spray it, 1 or 2 hours to let it dry, plus time to wet and observe your design

> ### WHAT YOU NEED
> sidewalk or other outdoor concrete area, such as a patio
> scissors
> masking tape
> hydrophobic spray (see p. 103 and safety tips, p. 7)
> OPTIONAL: stencil letters or other shaped objects with silhouettes that would look good in your design
> SAFETY EQUIPMENT: safety goggles, lab apron, face mask

Rainy forecast got you down? Before the rain falls, get something else down—a secret message or a game that will show up at the same time the storm does.

WATER WAY TO ACT

1

5

"The spray is afraid of the water so it's pushing it away."
—Audrey

2

"You're going to have to teach me how to hopscotch."
—Frank Young, U.S. Postal Service

OUR TRY

Liam and Audrey masked out a *Try This Extreme* hopscotch on the sidewalk using masking tape. We hoped for a rain shower but had to wet it with a watering can instead. We took turns hopscotching and even convinced the mail carrier to give it a try!

WHAT TO DO

1 PLAN YOUR MESSAGE or design. Create the design, laying materials down and, as necessary, keeping them in place with masking tape.

! 2 USING SAFETY EQUIPMENT, spray the area with hydrophobic spray. (See instructions on p. 103.)

3 LET DRY for several hours, leaving the objects in your design in place while il dries.

4 REMOVE the objects and masking tape.

5 WAIT FOR RAIN ... or wet your design with a watering can or by lightly spraying with a hose.

> WHAT TO EXPECT Water will expose your design! Passersby will be impressed!

> WHAT'S GOING ON Water rolls off the areas treated with hydrophobic spray into the areas that were not sprayed (the areas you covered or masked).

HERO'S ENGINE

Chemical reactions set things in motion—or does it take something more?

> **HOW LONG IT TAKES**
> 20 to 30 minutes

> **WHAT YOU NEED**
> soda can
> nail and hammer
> 1 yard (36 inches) of string
> fishing spinner
> stickers
> bucket of water
> something to hang your can from so that it can spin freely

This one had our wheels spinning and took several attempts, but eventually we got our engine in gear. Try our successful method, take another shot at the failures, or find another method.

WATER WAY TO ACT

OUR FIRST TRY

Our first group followed directions that said to mix dry ice with water inside film canisters. The idea was that the combination would create a reaction that would propel the engine. We got this wrong two ways. First, we didn't realize we needed to turn the hole so that the propellant shot out sideways. (We thought the key was to find the right relationship between the two holes, so each of us made our holes at different angles from each other.) The result: no spinning! As for the dry ice, although we got some exciting puffs of "steam" coming out of the hole, it didn't seem to generate enough energy to spin around.

NOTE: Dry ice is not part of the experiment instructions, but if you try to use it, please see the safety tips on p. 7.

DRY ICE *is frozen carbon dioxide. Its temperature is around -100°F. Handle it only with insulated mittens or protective gloves, **never bare hands.***

OUR SECOND TRY

This time we flattened the holes so they turned sideways, and, just to get fancy, we added fishing spinners. These are hooks with a swivel at the bottom to allow the thread to spin freely. Here's what happened: nothing. The dry ice and water didn't create much of a reaction, and the film canisters didn't spin.

OUR THIRD TRY

An Internet search turned up a method involving soda cans. First you had to poke a pinhole in the can to drain out the soda, because you weren't supposed to open the can the normal way. Try it sometime: The soda sprayed like wild. What a mess!

When it drained, we made another hole opposite the first and turned the holes to the side. We tied a string to the unopened flip top, and attached the other end to a fishing spinner. We were learning. We followed the directions to fill the can with water by pushing it under the surface of a bucket of water. Then we hung it quickly—but nothing happened. Our conclusion: First, you couldn't fill the can enough through the two holes on the sides; second, more water must be needed to make this engine run.

OUR FOURTH TRY

The last method seemed to make the most sense from the start. We kept it simple by opening the soda can the normal way, from the top, and draining the soda into a glass so we could drink it instead of wear it. We could still tie a string to the flip top, and we attached the other end to a fishing spinner to make it spin freely. What's more, we used nails instead of needles or pins to make holes. We made four holes, equally spaced around the lower edge of the can (where the pressure would be strongest) and turned toward the side. Liam turned his holes toward the right, and Gabriel, Audrey, and Cori each turned theirs left. Liam was just being different, and we don't know whether the direction of the holes affected the spinning. To fill the can, we just dunked it into a bucket and held it down until bubbles stopped coming up, indicating it was full.

For the first time, we really needed the stickers on each can in order to count the spins.
Our outcomes:
Liam—41
Gabriel—13
Cori—11
Audrey—3

Here's how to do the try that succeeded.

WHAT TO DO

1 OPEN THE CAN carefully, without breaking off the flip top. Empty the soda from the can.

! 2 USING A NAIL, make four holes near the bottom of the can, evenly spaced at 3, 6, 9, and 12 o'clock. First drive the nail directly in from the side, then remove it. Then, reinsert it halfway and push it so it is horizontal, flat against the can. This turns the hole to one side. Do the same with each hole, so they all turn in the same direction.

3 MAKE THE FLIP TOP STAND vertically from the can. Tie a string to the flip top. Tie the other end of the string to the loop at the bottom of a fishing spinner.

4 TIE ANOTHER PIECE of string from your overhang. Create a loop at the bottom. Open the clip of your fishing spinner so that it acts as a hook. You'll use the hook to attach to the loop coming from the overhang when the can is full.

5 PUT A STICKER on the side of the can. You'll count the spins by counting how many times the sticker goes by. (Otherwise, it could just be a blur!)

6 DUNK THE CAN into the bucket of water to fill it.

7 PICK UP THE CAN and quickly hook it onto the overhang string. Stand back!

WHAT TO EXPECT Water spurting from the holes should cause your can to spin. The number of spins may differ based on size and orientation of the holes, how easily the can is able to turn on the spinner, angle of the hang, and other factors. Experiment to get the maximum spin!

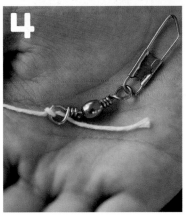

QUESTION THIS!

How could you heat the water inside a can to see if steam would make it spin more than cold water?

WHAT'S GOING ON Our Hero's Engine cans work because of the third law of motion—*For every action there is an equal and opposite reaction.* In other words, interactions create force. Our spinning cans work on the same principle as the aeolipile engine invented more than 2,000 years ago by Hero of Alexandria. His engine was a spinning copper sphere with thrust produced by heating water inside it. As the steam spurted out of the sphere, it spun. We didn't need heat to give our Hero's Engines a good spin. Placing the holes at the bottom of the cans ensures that the most water—and the water with the greatest pressure—is spilling out through the holes. Once the water drains out, the thrust ends and the spinning stops.

"Wait until the bubbles stop before you take the can out of the water to spin, then you'll know it's full."
—Cori

SCAREDY SAND

Who ever heard of sand that's scared of water?

SIMPLE

WHO YOU NEED

GRAB A GROWN-UP

SUPERVISION: SPRAYING CHEMICALS

CONCEPTS

CHEMISTRY, BEHAVIOR OF WATER, BEHAVIOR OF SAND, SOLIDS, LIQUIDS

> #### HOW LONG IT TAKES
> 10 minutes one day, then a day to dry, and an hour or two the next day for experimentation/exploration

> #### WHAT YOU NEED
> sand (from beach) or colored craft sand (We bought our colored sand at a craft store.)
> NOTE: You can do this with any sand, but having sand in different colors makes it easier to experiment with combining them.
> 4 containers with lids for sand
> hydrophobic spray (see box on p. 103 and safety tips, p. 7)
> water
> OPTIONAL: smaller containers for pouring, spoons, straws
> SAFETY EQUIPMENT: safety goggles, face mask, lab apron

36

Hydrophobic spray changes the behavior of water—but what will it do to sand? Explore the possibilities, mix and match, then figure out what's happening.

1

2

3a

> "It's like a paste, folding on top of each other."
> —Karisa (hydrophobic sand in water)

> "Bubbles are coming out of the untreated sand. It all settled to the bottom and didn't mix with each other."
> —Jameer (treated and untreated sand in the same water)

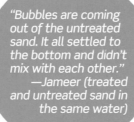

3c

WHAT TO DO

1 DIVIDE YOUR SAMPLE sand and separate it into containers. We think it's ideal to use two different colors of sand for a total of four samples—one in each color sprayed and one in each color not sprayed.

! ⯈ 2 SPRAY ONE CONTAINER of each color sand with hydrophobic spray (see instructions on p. 103), repeating the procedure three times, stirring between sprays. Leave the second container of each color sand unsprayed. Put lids on both, and let them dry for at least 24 hours.

3 EXPERIMENT WITH your sand. Here are a few options. You'll probably come up with more as you play around.

- **a** Work with one color. Divide each container in two so that you have four samples—two sprayed and two unsprayed. Add water to one sprayed sample and one unsprayed sample. Compare. Try different combinations, for example combining wet sprayed sand with wet unsprayed sand.

- **b** Combine dry sprayed sand of one color with dry unsprayed sand of another color. Is it possible to separate them again?

- **c** Combine colors to see what new colors are formed—or not.

- **d** Compare wet and dry sprayed and unsprayed sand.

- **e** See how sprayed sand behaves in narrow cups compared with wet sand.

⯈ WHAT TO EXPECT You'll find that hydrophobic sand behaves oddly compared to waterlogged sand.

⯈ WHAT'S GOING ON Most of the hydrophobic sand will repel water even as it is immersed in and surrounded by it. So it will look and behave differently from the unsprayed sand. Some grains of sand may have more coating than others, so you'll get a range of behaviors when the sand is combined with water or untreated sand.

BOTTLE WON'T POUR

A party trick or serious science? Both!

SAFETY CHECK

SIMPLE

WHO YOU NEED

JUST YOU

SUPERVISION: GLASS BOTTLE

CONCEPTS

Surface tension, water cohesion, liquids, solids

HOW LONG IT TAKES
10 minutes

WHAT YOU NEED
empty glass soda bottle or other glass bottle with narrow neck
water
small piece of screen (window screen is perfect) about 3 x 3 inches
rubber band
toothpick
OPTIONAL: bucket or sink to do this over, but you can do it outside, too

Simple and strange, this experiment reveals a secret power of water. Experience it, then try to explain it—and figure out how water uses this superpower.

WHAT TO DO

1 FILL the bottle with water.

2 WRAP THE SCREEN tightly over the mouth of the bottle, smoothing out wrinkles. Fasten with rubber band.

3 FLIP THE BOTTLE upside down quickly.

> WHAT TO EXPECT The water will not pour from the bottle.

> WHAT'S GOING ON What's the big idea? Surface tension and cohesion are the main concepts here. Water molecules cohere, sticking together. This cohesion creates surface tension, an invisible skin on water that is broken sharply when it's pierced—but the hole quickly mends because the molecules pull together to mend the skin. Water poured out slowly at an angle moves uniformly, following gravity, but the screen is enough to keep the surface tension intact if the bottle is inverted quickly. For more, see Bonus.

> GLITCH Water pours out? Try flipping the bottle over faster. Otherwise, you may need to try a screen with different-size mesh.

> TWEAKS AND TWISTS We thought back to how dish detergent affected milk and decided to try adding a drop to our bottle. The soap didn't break the surface tension enough to let the bottle pour.

QUESTION THIS!

How does this experiment relate to why ketchup won't pour from a bottle? Maybe you've heard how hitting a bottle of ketchup on the side makes the ketchup pour; we tried this with our bottle that wouldn't pour. Water spurted out briefly, then stopped. What happens when you try?

"When the water is sticking together it's because of cohesion. In a company everyone has to work together! That's cohesion. When something hits the water, it hits the tension first and then it goes underwater."
—Sofia

OUR TRY

When Jameer inserted a toothpick, one drip would come out, but quickly the surface tension "skin" would mend up the hole (said Sofia) and no more water would come out.

"When I stick a toothpick in, a drop of water comes down and then bubbles go up inside the bottle. I wonder if I'm not sticking it in far enough."
—Jameer

BONUS

Take the screen off and place it in a bucket of water. What happens? The results demonstrate the same cohesion we saw in our experiment. Water fills the spaces in the mesh, creating a membrane.

HOT STUFF

There are many sources of heat, some obvious and maybe some unexpected. Amazing experiments can be done when you heat things up! Use heat from an electric bulb, microwave heat, a heat wave, or just a perfect summer day to fuel projects that will impress you to a high degree.

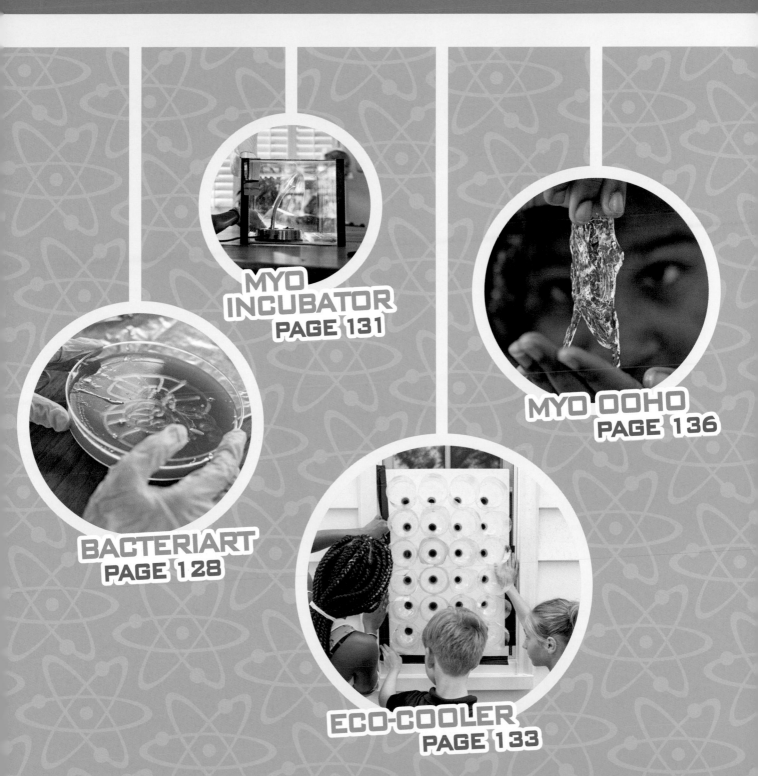

MYO
INCUBATOR
PAGE 131

MYO OOHO
PAGE 136

BACTERIART
PAGE 128

ECO-COOLER
PAGE 133

PEEPS ZAP

What's in your kitchen and works at the speed of light?

SAFETY CHECK

DIFFICULT

WHO YOU NEED

GRAB A GROWN-UP

SUPERVISION: MICROWAVE COOKING

CONCEPTS

PHYSICS, WAVES, GEOMETRY, MATHEMATICS

HOW LONG IT TAKES
One hour

WHAT YOU NEED
microwave oven large enough to accommodate a baking dish
glass baking dish
about 10 packages of marshmallow Peeps
toothpicks
ruler
calculator or smartphone calculator app
laptop or smartphone with Internet connection
OPTIONAL: bunny ears

A sticky problem that gets to the heart of physics, this one involves experimentation, measurement, and a bit of math.

1 USE THE MELTING RATE of microwaved marshmallow Peeps to find the approximate speed of light.

- **a** First, figure out the lowest, slowest way to cook with your microwave. To do this, you may need to sacrifice a few peeps. Careful: They can explode in the microwave. Once you have determined how to cook low and slow, continue.

- **b** Check the label on the interior of your oven to find the frequency of the microwaves used to heat. This measurement appears in megahertz (MHz). Ours was 2450 MHz.

- **NOTE:** The speed at which a wave travels is found by multiplying its frequency by the length of the wave (the distance between two wave peaks), also called wavelength. Microwaves move at about the same speed as light, so if you can find the speed of your microwave oven's waves, you can approximate the speed of light.

2 TAKE the rotating device out of the microwave. You don't want your Peeps to turn while they're cooking.

3 PACK YOUR DISH solidly and evenly with marshmallow Peeps.

! 4 COOK YOUR PEEPS at low for about 90 seconds.

! 5 TAKE THE DISH OUT of the microwave and look at the Peeps closely. You will notice that some spots seem more melted than others. Use a toothpick to find an area that seems particularly well melted and stick the toothpick in to mark the spot. Continue doing this until you have about 10 extra-melty spots tagged with toothpicks.

Continued on next page

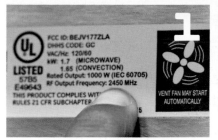

> *"For some reason the bunnies are weak."*
> —Kamari

HOT STUFF

6

7

8

WHAT TO DO

6 USE A RULER to measure the distance between the toothpicks. Make a list of these distances and average them. To calculate the average, first add all the distances together. Then divide by the number of distances. Now you have the wavelength, in inches or centimeters.

7 USE THE INTERNET to find a converter from megahertz (MHz) to inches or centimeters (cm) per second. Convert your frequency to inches or cm per second. For example, our frequency 2450 MHz = 2,450,000,000 inches per second (2.45 billion inches per second)

8 MULTIPLY the newly converted frequency by the wavelength. For example, 2,450,000,000 x 4.86 = 11,907,000,000 inches per second.

BUT speed of light is usually measured in miles or kilometers per hour. How many inches or centimeters is your speed per second? Convert your inches or centimeters per second to miles or kilometers an hour. One mile is 63,360 inches. One kilometer is 100,000 cm.

QUESTION THIS!

How are microwaves and light waves different? How are they similar?

WHAT TO EXPECT Your calculations should bring your answer close to the speed of light, close being a relative term. We think a 30 million mph error brought us pretty close!

WHAT'S GOING ON Like light, microwaves are a kind of electromagnetic wave. They travel not in straight lines but in a pattern of curves called waves. The difference between kinds of light wave is their speed, wavelength, and frequency. The reason microwave ovens have rotating plates is that microwaves bounce around inside the oven, creating hot and cold spots; the rotation evens out this effect to some degree. Taking out the rotator lets you see exactly which spots in the dish of Peeps receive the strongest microwave signals.

OUR TRY

We used a combination of Peeps bunnies and chicks, which have different shapes, as you may know. We attempted to layer them evenly, but the bunnies may have accounted for some of the error in our experiment. Our calculation came out to just under 700,000,000 miles per hour. Pretty close to the actual speed of light!

The actual speed of light is 670, 616, 629 mph, or 1,079,252,847.32 kph.

BACKYARD BIOBLITZ

Yes, in YOUR backyard!

CONCEPTS

BIOLOGY, ECOLOGY, SCIENTIFIC METHODS

HOW LONG IT TAKES

24 hours, plus identification time

WHAT YOU NEED

sheet
clothesline and clothespins
black light
paper or plastic cups
small garden trowel or golf-hole cutter
4 rocks, each the size of a golf ball
1 flat rock or piece of bark about the size of your hand or larger
bait (see bait list on p.123)
jars
screen
rubber bands
OPTIONAL: small bug net, tweezers, identification guides (books or online), screen, rubber bands

A cross the world, people conduct bioblitzes in their parks. But you can conduct a bioblitz anywhere by counting living things. This one focuses on bugs.

INSIDER INFO:
What can you find with a backyard bioblitz? Gary Hevel, a retired entomologist from the Smithsonian Institution Museum of Natural History, told us he has been conducting bioblitzes in his backyard in Silver Spring, Maryland, U.S.A., for 60 years. In that time he has identified more than 4,500 insect species, including 1,000 beetles, 700 moths, and a new species of fly, as well as bugs that were not known to inhabit the Western Hemisphere.

WHAT TO DO

METHOD 1:
Flying Bug Trap/**Daytime**

1 DURING THE DAY, use an existing clothesline or tie line between two uprights (such as two trees or between two posts).

2 USE CLOTHESPINS to attach a sheet to the clothesline.

3 GATHER the bottom of the sheet loosely into a jar so that the sheet forms a funnel.

> WHAT TO EXPECT Flying insects land on the sheet and slide down into the jar or can be shaken down into the jar out of their entrapment in the folds of the sheet.

METHOD 2:
Flying Bug Trap/**Nighttime**

1 WHEN IT'S DARK OUTSIDE, use the sheet attached to the clothesline. Pull the sheet out of the jar and spread the bottom of it on the ground so that there's a flap about a foot (12 inches) wide lying flat on the ground. Note that you may need to pin the top of the clothesline differently to allow this, or you may need to lower the clothesline slightly. Set the jar aside.

2 SET UP a black light on the ground on the side opposite the sheet flap, so that it shines up onto the sheet.

> WHAT TO EXPECT Insects attracted to light and to ultraviolet light will land or crawl onto your sheet. The flap is to allow the crawlers to get to the lighted area of the sheet from the ground.

Method 1
1

Method 3
1

2b

3

2d

> "They're red ants, they've got a red and yellow thing that looks like a stinger. Ew, I'm touching all that gunky bait. There's no way I'm going to catch one of these! I've got it, it's in! Oh! I got an ant!"
>
> —Gabrielle, using "wheast" as bait

METHOD 3:
Pitfalls

1 USE PLASTIC OR PAPER CUPS. Dig a hole deep enough to accommodate the cup so that the lip falls below the edge of the hole. Build dirt up over the lip so that bugs crawling in won't be stopped by the lip.

2 BAIT YOUR PITFALL. Here are some suggested baits and the bugs that are said to be attracted to them:

- **a** sugar water (water with a lot of sugar in it): attracts flies
- **b** wheast (equal parts sugar and yeast, plus small amount of water): attracts beetles and ladybugs
- **c** fruit, including rotting bananas, watermelon, oranges: attracts butterflies
- **d** peanut butter: attracts ants
- **e** perfume: attracts wasps and other stinging insects
- **f** rotting fish: attracts beetles

3 COVER YOUR PITFALL. Use four rocks about the size of a golf ball and a flat rock or flat piece of bark to make a lid that is raised above the level of the top of the pitfall. Covering the pitfall makes it more appealing to many bugs, and may keep out amphibians (snakes, turtles, frogs, toads) that may be attracted to the bugs. Note: Certain bugs, such as butterflies, may be more attracted to an open pitfall, but this means you have to be vigilant to keep other critters from falling in.

WHAT TO EXPECT Insects, slugs, snails, arachnids, and others will creep or fly into your pitfall, but are they the ones you were trying to attract?

Continued on next page

a

b

"The thrill is still there. I am still attempting to find key species in my backyard, including a Luna moth, zebra swallowtail butterfly, a caterpillar hunter beetle, and a big popular sphinx moth, to name but a few."
—Gary Hevel, retired Smithsonian Institution entomologist who advised us on our bioblitz and who has conducted them in his Maryland backyard for decades.

"A slug is coming in, it's attracted to the peanut butter, and black ants. This ant has peanut butter in his mouth. He's stuck in the slug's slime."
—Alex

BONUS

GATHER BUGS

- **a** Prepare jars to hold bugs: Cut pieces of screen and use a rubber band to secure them to your jars, or, if you use Mason jars, screw on the outer piece of the lid over the screen.

- **b** You may pull the cup out of your pitfall and carefully dump your bugs into a jar, or use tweezers or a pencil to gently brush them into your hand, onto a card, or into a cup or jar or a small bug net.

- **c** Place the bugs in a jar along with some of the food they were eating.

- **d** Identify your bugs using online guides or insect guide books, such as National Geographic Kids *Ultimate Explorer Field Guide: Insects.*

- **e** When you are done, gently release the bugs back where you found them.

c

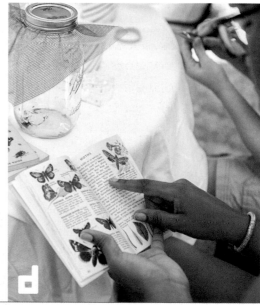

d

LIQUID LENS

What lurks beneath the surface of a neighborhood pond?

CONCEPTS

BIOLOGY, MICROSCOPY, PROPERTIES OF LIGHT

HOW LONG IT TAKES

An hour, including collection time

WHAT YOU NEED

white wall, screen, or foam board
laser pointer 532 nm/100 watts or more
2 binder clips (You can use a third binder clip to hold the toothpick horizontally; or you can use a heavy book, but it might get wet.)
2 rubber bands for laser pointer stand
wooden toothpick or shish kebab skewer
small dish or plastic lid to catch drips
water from pond or puddle
bucket or collection jar
eyedropper
dark or darkened room
OPTIONAL: spray bottle, nitrile gloves for handling water sample
SAFETY ADVICE: Never look into the light coming from the laser pointer!

Dramatic and beautiful, this experiment rewards you for the effort you take to find the liveliest water in nature—whether it's in a pond or a puddle.

WHAT TO DO

1 SET UP your projection area as follows:

- **a** You'll need a vertical white screen on which to project. (We set a sheet of white foam core on a kitchen counter.)

- **b** About 6 feet from the screen, set up your laser: Press down the "ears" of two binder clips and set the clips on the flat side. Use these to make front and back rests for your laser pointer. Use rubber bands to secure the laser pointer to each rest.

- **c** Aim the laser at the center of the screen.

- **d** Position the toothpick horizontally so that its point sits right in the beam of the laser pointer. Use a binder clip, pile of books, adjustable wrench, whatever you need to secure the toothpick in position.

- **e** Set a small dish or lid beneath the toothpick to catch drips. We positioned our laser and toothpick setups on the island in the kitchen opposite the "screen" on the counter.

! 2 GATHER WATER from a pond or puddle into a clean jar or bucket. Bring the sample to the projection area.

3 USE THE EYEDROPPER to gather water from the sample and drip it onto the toothpick so that the drop dangles from the toothpick without dropping. (This sounds harder than it actually is. If the toothpick is horizontal, the drop should hang on pretty well. If it drops, just try another. You may need several drops over the course of this experiment.)

! 4 SHINE THE LASER POINTER through the drop of water onto the white backdrop. You may need to adjust the distance between the laser and the drop of water to get a clear image on your projection screen.
WARNING: *Never point a laser into someone's eyes!*

1d

2

3-4

"You can see through them to the ones behind."
—Karisa

"It's like a snow globe!"
—Sofia

"Oh there it is, hold on! I see a whole city of those little molecules!"
—Myrrh

> **WHAT TO EXPECT** The shadows of living microbes will be projected onto the screen, allowing you to observe them.

> **WHAT'S GOING ON** The combination of the water and the laser light, and the distance to the projection screen magnify the shadows of the microbes so that they are visible.

BONUS

Examine your sample with the digital microscope you made on page 43 (MYO Digital Microscope).

OUR TRY

The laser projected through the drop and onto the wall, showing a multitude of swimming, one-celled (-looking) microbes. They would settle down and not move, but could get aroused again into action by touching the drop with a toothpick. We videotaped this, too.

QUESTION THIS!

Compare samples from two areas. What makes the microbes in one area different in size, shape, or activity from others? Why are the microbes sometimes more active than at other times? What would these microbes look like under a microscope?

BACTERIART

Grow yourself some artwork when you paint with bacteria.

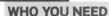

CONCEPTS

MICROBIOLOGY, SCIENTIFIC METHODS

HOW LONG IT TAKES

3 to 4 days

WHAT YOU NEED

growth medium (see Step 1)
saucepan
petri dishes
bouillon and 2 teaspoons sugar
cutting board
bleach solution, 1 part bleach to 3 parts water (see safety tips, p. 7)
rubbing alcohol and gauze
nitrile gloves and lab aprons
cotton swabs such as Q-Tips
Ziploc bags (must fit around petri dishes)

If you feed it, it will grow. Create a food source for bacteria, and get them to grow in a pattern of your design.

WHAT TO DO

! **1 HAVE AN ADULT HELP** you prepare growth medium.

- **a** commercially bought agar: Place jar in saucepan full of water to same level as the agar in the jar. Loosen cap slightly. Heat pot until agar is completely melted, could be 30 minutes. Let cool 15 minutes. We bought ours from a science classroom supply company along with our petri dishes.

- **b** use agar agar from grocery store: Per petri dish, 1 cup water, 1 tablespoon agar agar*, 1 teaspoon (or one cube) bouillon, 2 teaspoons sugar. Bring to a boil, stirring every minute. Remove from heat and cover, cool 15 minutes.

! **2 IN A WELL-VENTILATED AREA,** away from heat sources, sterilize the cutting board and the edge of your medium container. Use the bleach solution and gauze on the cutting board. Use rubbing alcohol and gauze on the edges of the saucepan or medium jar.

3 SET UP TWO OR THREE petri dishes on the cutting board. Take the lid off each dish by sliding it to the side so it is one-third or half open, then pour in growth medium until the dish is about half full and close the lid. Let the dishes cool. You can store them in the refrigerator until you are ready to establish your bacteria cultures.

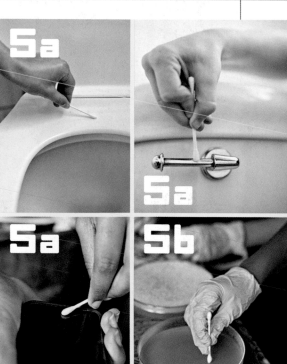

4 BEFORE establishing cultures, shake any condensation from the lids of your petri dishes.

5 ESTABLISH CULTURES:

- **a** Use a fresh, sterile cotton swab to get cultures from surfaces, such as a toilet.

- **b** In the first petri dish, draw gently with the swab in the surface of the agar and close the lid.

Continued on next page

HOT STUFF

WHAT TO DO

5 ESTABLISH CULTURES:

- **c** In a second dish, use another swab (from your pet's paw or other surface) to draw a paw print or other design in the agar, then close the lid.

6 LABEL your Ziploc bags with the source of the culture. Insert the petri dish in the bag and close.

7 WAIT 72 HOURS, keeping your petri dishes at about 90°F. This is easy enough to do in Washington, D.C., in July, as we did!

8 EXAMINE your cultures.

9 KILL YOUR CULTURES by dumping the petri dishes into bleach solution.

"Could you smash microbes with your hand?"
—Gabrielle

OUR PREDICTIONS

Which of our cultures will have the most bacteria grow?

- Gabrielle: "toilet seat"
- David: "the dog's paw"
- Mychal-Jael: "The phone? No, scratch that. Maybe the toilet, because there are multiple people using it, but if it's your phone it's just you using it."
- Alex: "the dog's paw"

OUR TRY

We cultured the toilet seat, the toilet handle, the screen of Karen's cell phone, and Rosie's paw.

MYO INCUBATOR

Want to make your own incubator? How hot!

CONCEPTS

ENGINEERING, BIOLOGY, MICROBIOLOGY, LAB PROCEDURE

> **HOW LONG IT TAKES**
> One hour

> **WHAT YOU NEED**
> aquarium (doesn't have to be watertight)
> sheets of plastic (The hardware store sells this by the yard.)
> duct tape
> desk lamp
> thermometer
> OPTIONAL: extension cord, dimmer

Build your own incubator using an old aquarium and a desk lamp to speed up growing bacteriart—or to add warmth to any experiment.

WHAT TO DO

1 TURN the aquarium on its side so the top opening faces sideways.

2 CUT A SHEET of plastic 2 inches longer than the top opening. Duct tape it on at the top so that the bottom has a flap that sits on your table.

3 PLUG IN the desk lamp and put it inside the aquarium.

4 POSITION the thermometer so that you can see it from outside the aquarium.

5 YOU CAN TURN the light on and off or adjust the plastic covering to allow cool air in, to maintain a temperature of about 90°F. You can also attach a dimmer to your light to adjust the temperature.

> **WHAT TO EXPECT** The enclosed desk lamp will create a warm growing environment.

> **WHAT'S GOING ON** The warmth of the electric light heats the air inside the aquarium. The plastic sheet helps keep warm air in and cold air out.

ECO-COOLER

How do you cool a house without electricity?

CONCEPTS

THERMODYNAMICS, PHYSICS, ENGINEERING

> ### HOW LONG IT TAKES
> A few hours, not counting the time it takes to gather bottles

> ### WHAT YOU NEED
> window
> ¼-inch foam core, 20 x 30 inches
> craft or X-Acto knife
> gaffer's tape or duct tape
> 24 2-L soda bottles, clean, empty, with caps
> ruler
> pencil or marker
> compass
> pipe cutter for cutting the tops off lids
> OPTIONAL: T-square, fan

In the age of the Internet, sharing an invention has power. In this project, we adapt a design that was shared with the hope of helping people without electricity cool their homes.

WHAT TO DO

1 MAKE the Eco-Cooler

- **a** Select a window and cut your foam core to fit it, if needed. You will tape the Eco-Cooler to the window's edges. Choose a different window or use larger foam core (and more bottles) if needed to get a close fit.

  b Cut the bottle in half and measure the radius (about 4 inches for a 2-liter bottle). Trace the cut bottle as a stencil to fit as many bottles on the board as possible or use a compass (as shown) to draw circles where the bottles will fit. Then flip the bottle and trace its neck (usually one inch) in the center of each stencil. Cut out the one-inch hole for the bottle neck.

  c With the help of a grown-up, use the pipe cutter to trim off the top of each cap. Make sure the lid is still on (because it's easier to cut this way).

- **d** For each bottle:
  Cut the bottom half off (use it to make string; see Bottle of String, p. 96). Push the neck through the hole in the board. Screw the cap back on the other side to hold the bottle in place.

"What if the air outside was going through the small end of the bottle into the house. Would it make the air warmer?"
—Mychal-Jael

INSIDER INFO:
The Eco-Cooler was devised to help cool corrugated tin houses without electricity in the hot country of Bangladesh. The designers made their design available to the public to make it easier for people to get the cool air they need. You wouldn't typically make the Eco-Cooler out of foam core but would use composite board or plywood. Our version is not meant to be used to cool a house for real; we used foam core to make it easier to cut the holes for the bottles, so we could demonstrate the principles of the design and see how well it serves to cool air.

WHAT TO DO

2 SET IT UP and test it. Stand or tape the Eco-Cooler in the window with the necks pointing into the house and the bottoms of the bottles facing out.

> **WHAT TO EXPECT** The air coming through the bottles will be cooler than the air around it.

> **WHAT'S GOING ON** Try blowing on your hand with your mouth wide open. Now purse your lips and blow on your hand. Which method cools the air? The Eco-Cooler makes use of this principle, known as the Venturi effect. The Venturi effect describes what happens when a fluid is forced through a narrow space, so that the pressure decreases—and the velocity increases.
>
> NOTE: If you take a look at comments online about this, you'll see a lot of discussion about whether the Venturi effect is what's happening—or whether other factors are cooling the air (the designers claim a temperature drop of up to 5°C/9°F).

> **CONSIDER THIS** Notice how the air coming through the Eco-Cooler feels compared to air coming through a window without an Eco-Cooler. Optional: Set up a fan outside to mimic other weather conditions. What difference does it make?

MYO OOHO

Sick of plastic bottles? We are. Here's an invention: a biodegradable, edible water bottle that's a new way to store and carry water.

"It feels like Jell-O!"
—Gabrielle

SAFETY CHECK

DIFFICULT

WHO YOU NEED

GRAB A GROWN-UP & FRIEND

SUPERVISION: HAND BLENDER

CONCEPTS

CHEMISTRY, PHYSICS

> > **HOW LONG IT TAKES**
One hour

> **WHAT YOU NEED**
3 to 6 glass bowls: 1 medium, 1 large, 1 to 4 small
measuring spoons and cups
sodium alginate (a substance made from seaweed, used to thicken and bind)
hand blender
water flavor enhancer (liquid, e.g., Mio)
calcium lactate (a type of salt used in foods such as baking powder)
ladle or slotted spoon

INSIDER INFO: Americans use 50 billion plastic water bottles a year.

Another forward-thinking innovation, designed to help the environment, gave us this project. It may just have been everyone's favorite.

OOHO

is a play on H$_2$O, the chemical formula for water. Some people capitalize all the letters, but we've seen it written both ways.

WHAT TO DO

1 IN THE MEDIUM-SIZE BOWL, make a sodium alginate solution: Mix 1½ cup drinking water, ½ teaspoon sodium alginate.

! 2 BLEND one minute, then let rest 15–20 minutes until there are no bubbles.

3 DIVIDE the sodium alginate solution into smaller bowls and stir a squirt of Mio or a similar drink mix into each. Or just add one color to your bowl or even clear water. Note: it will be harder to see the OOHO with clear water, but it's an option.

4 IN LARGE BOWL, combine 4 cups of water plus 2 teaspoons of calcium lactate.

5 SLOWLY SLIDE the round-bottom spoon into the sodium alginate solution, then gently roll the blob out of it into the calcium lactate solution in the large bowl.

6 IN ABOUT 30 SECONDS you'll see a pale blob in the water. Leave it there for 3–4 minutes. Then transfer it to a small bowl of clear water to rinse off. Finally, transfer to a dish. You can make several OOHOs at once.

> **WHAT TO EXPECT** Your OOHOs will feel like gelatinous water bubbles, and taste like the flavored drops or just plain water.

> **WHAT'S GOING ON** Sodium alginate is derived from seaweed (algae). When combined with calcium lactate, it forms a biodegradable membrane that contains water.

"Weird, it's like oobleck!"
—Alex

"What if you had a cookie cutter, could you make it a perfect shape?"
—Mychal-Jael

3 BONUS MINI-EXPERIMENTS!

Here are some cool experiments you can do whenever you have a little extra time. They are all quick and produce amazing results. Dive in!

1 MAKE A CAMERA

> **HOW LONG IT TAKES**
30 minutes

> **WHAT YOU NEED**
sharp pencil
empty shoe box with a lid
X-Acto knife (ask an adult)
scissors
ruler
wax paper
tape
blanket and lamp

Pinhole cameras were one of the earliest types of cameras. They use the principle of "camera obscura," in which light travels through a small hole in a dark box to form a picture. It's the same science that today's cameras use.

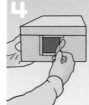

WHAT TO DO

1 USE the point of a sharp pencil to punch a hole in one of the shorter ends of the shoe box.

2 ASK AN ADULT to use an X-Acto knife to cut a square in the opposite end of the box, directly across from the hole. The square should measure 2 inches on each side.

3 USE scissors to cut a square of wax paper that measures 3 inches on each side.

4 PLACE the wax paper directly over the square you cut in the box. Tape the edges of the wax paper to the box.

5 TAKE the camera box to a dimly lit room and turn on a lamp. Stand about 5 feet from the lamp.

6 COVER your head and pinhole camera with a blanket. Be sure that the end with the wax paper is facing you and the end with the pinhole is facing the lamp.

7 HOLD your pinhole camera at arms length from your face and aim it at the lamp. Keep it steady until you see an upside-down image of the lamp.

2 MAKE A GROOVY LAVA LAMP

Using stuff you probably have lying around the kitchen, you and your family can make your very own lava lamp and learn a bit of science while doing it!

HOW LONG IT TAKES
15 minutes

WHAT YOU NEED
clear jar with lid
water
food coloring
glitter
vegetable oil
salt
flashlight

WHAT TO DO

1 FILL the jar three-quarters full of water. Add drops of food coloring until you like the color you see. A few drops go a long way! Sprinkle in glitter for extra sparkle.

2 FILL the jar almost to the top with the oil and let the mixture separate.

3 POUR salt into the jar until you see the cool lava lamp effect. When the bubbles stop, add more salt to see it again.

4 SHINE a flashlight behind the jar to watch your lava lamp really glow!

3 BOTTLED MUSIC

Changing the amounts of air and water in the bottles lets you change the pitch—how high or low the sound is. When you blow across the tops of the bottles, you are making the air inside vibrate. In bottles with more air, vibrations are slower, so the pitch is lower.

HOW LONG IT TAKES
15 minutes

WHAT YOU NEED
5 identical glass or plastic bottles
water

WHAT TO DO

1 FILL the bottles with varying amounts of water.

2 ARRANGE the bottles in order from least to most full.

3 BLOW across the top of each bottle and compare the different sounds you make.

THE QUESTION

Not everything can be shaped into a science fair project, but most things can—if they include a phenomenon that can be observed given the right conditions.

> ### SOME PHENOMENA IN THIS BOOK:

IF I MIX MILK, FOOD COLORING, and dish soap in a baking dish, the mixture will marbleize and combine the colors, producing an amazing pattern (p. 82).

IF THE EYE SEES a hand holding an object, it will be fooled seeing that object as smaller than the hand (p. 92).

IF WARM AIR BLOWS from a large space through a small space, it will cool (p. 133).

So, what can you do with each of these phenomena to make them into science fair projects?

Ask yourself a few questions: For example, in the first phenomenon, the one about mixing colors, you need multiple colors.

> > **What are the conditions involved in this phenomenon?**

> **What can be tested, changed, or compared?**

You could try doing the experiment with a baking dish that's a different shape to see what happens. Here are a few more questions to shape the experiment in different ways.

Science Fair Question: Can I change the speed of the color/milk/soap reaction?

Science Fair Question: How much temperature change will air passing through an Eco-Cooler demonstrate?

Science Fair Question: How can camera angles change apparent size relationships?

THE EXPERIMENT

Once you have narrowed down your topic and come up with your question, consider what you could do as an experiment. Here are the pieces of the experiment that you need to have in place for the science fair.

> HYPOTHESIS **What you think will happen.**

For example, your hypothesis could be that the Eco-Cooler will lower air temperature.

> BACKGROUND RESEARCH: **Information about your topic that would be good to know before you start, or that you need to find as you go along.**

For example, you might do research about different methods for cooling air, or about the Venturi effect (see p. 135).

(see p. 135)

> MATERIALS: **What you need to do your experiment.**

For example, soda bottles, board, and cutting tools.

> PROCEDURE: **What you'll do for this experiment.**

For example, you'll want to identify a window in which to place your Eco-Cooler as a demonstration and to alter the plans to make an Eco-Cooler that will fit there snugly—or to come up with a way to demonstrate your Eco-Cooler on-site at the science fair or through video.

RESULTS: The data you find when you do your experiment. It's vital to consider this before you start.

For example, you're going to take the temperature outside and inside the window. Consider whether it would be best to do this once or at different times of day or under different weather conditions. Consider also whether you might try the Eco-Cooler in different windows in your house to see how positioning affects them. Then plan your procedure, including the data you're gathering.

CONCLUSION: What you find— your data—should lead you to a new understanding of the situation you're exploring and give you an answer to the question you began with.

Say you find that the Eco-Cooler only makes a difference on days when the temperature outside your house is 20 degrees (or more) hotter than inside it. You may realize that a significant difference in temperature drives the effectivity of the Eco-Cooler.

FUTURE INDICATIONS: These are the questions your work raises.

Then you may set out to determine what the pattern of the Eco-Cooler's effectiveness is like. For instance, for each additional 10 degrees outside, what is the difference in temperature inside? Is there any pattern change at all?

WHAT'S NEXT? You still haven't started yet, but before you do, consider the end product.

The next few pages include some things you're going to need to present to your teacher and/or science fair committee and some advice on how to make the experiments shine.

TIP

Consider your project backward. You know what your experiment is going to be, and you know you're going to need a demonstration and/or poster and presentation. What parts will you need to complete? Before you start, plan on filling in the blanks by looking for exactly what you need as you work forward. For example, if you think your science fair booth would be stronger if you included a diagram of your experiment, plan on drawing one in your lab notes before you begin.

THE NOTES

Your laboratory notebook should be clear, neat, and well-organized. You can lay it out before you begin, leaving yourself extra space for each area you want to complete.

> **Number the pages, and date each page as you work on your project.**

In your book, list the goals of your project and the different jobs you have to do to complete it. Then break down each job into steps, and document (take notes on) what you do as you complete each step. Add drawings and photographs, and keep note of materials and procedures you used. You might think this is silly, because you're the one doing things, following directions carefully. But if you note each thing you're doing, the date and time you do it, and what you find at each step, this will translate easily into your write-up and presentations. It will make it easier for you to remember not only what you did and when you did it but what you felt and thought as you went along.

> **Organize your data-gathering in tables and charts.**

Say you are testing three subjects to see how they respond to your variables. For example, you are doing Bacteriart on three petri dishes. For each petri dish, make a table showing where the swab was gathered, how long it was cultured

for, and the characteristics of each culture. As you go through the process of the experiment, all you'll have to do is fill in the blanks in your table. Simple!

In your notes, include what you think about the data and whether they reflect your expectations before you started.

> **Keep note of mistakes or complications or problems that arise as you work.**

Include these issues in your write-up as you explain the situations that may have affected your results. If possible, repeat your experiment to see if you can amend the situation, but include the first trials in your report.

TRY THIS!

THE WRITE-UP

One-third of most science fair grades will come from the paper, write-up, or report you write about your experiment or project.

CONSIDER YOUR EXPERIENCE and create a project title. This can be a word, phrase, or question that shows what you learned from your experience or shows what you were curious about when you started.

BEGIN with an abstract, a brief description of the project and summary of your experiment and findings. An abstract is like a trailer for a film: It tells people about the project and makes them want to know more.

CREATE a table of contents that reflects the pieces of your project. (This will help you structure your paper. Plan the parts of your paper first, then just fill in what is needed.)

WRITE your introduction to give the purpose of your work. (Why did you choose this project?) State what you hoped to discover and give your hypothesis.

TELL about the research you did to find out more about your topic, procedure, method, and materials. The review of literature is where to put information about others who have worked on your question, what they learned or did, and how their work relates to yours.

DESCRIBE your process. List and describe your materials, the steps in your procedure, and your results. This may be the longest part of your paper, written in careful detail so that another scientist could follow your process the way a cook follows a recipe.

SHOW your raw data—the measurements or other numbers—just as you found them. You may include excerpts from your notes, including tables and calculations.

ORGANIZE your data. Add tables or graphs that make it easy to see what your data told you. Use Microsoft Excel or another graphing program.

WRITE your conclusion. This tells what you found out by doing your experiment. Circle back to your hypothesis, and discuss whether the result of your experiment agreed with your hypothesis.

SYNTHESIZE future indications. State the questions your work raised. Talk about future experiments that might be—or must be—done before this subject can be fully understood.

LIST your sources. Create a clear and specific bibliography or "works cited" page.

Backyard Bio Blitz
1.) Gabrielle / sugar with yeast
3. Mychal / Wine / Su...

TRY THIS!

AT THE SCIENCE FAIR

THE BOOTH

What's in your booth? Here's another planning-backward tip: Think about what you'll want to talk about and show people as you stand in your booth at the science fair.

THE TABLE: Try to include things—besides your poster or display board—that help a viewer "see" your lab. Include your laboratory notebook and some of your materials. If it's possible to share some of the procedures or findings in physical form at your table, do so.

THE DEMONSTRATION: You can't often replicate your whole experiment in your science fair booth, but you may be able to show some aspect of it. For example, you could have containers on display with biofilm growing in several stages. Or how about some biofilm under a dissecting microscope for visitors to view? This helps bring your experiment to life.

> POSTER TIPS

Use a headline and smaller sub-heads to chunk up your information. This allows a viewer to scan your poster and easily see what your project is about without having to read every detail.

Use a big font so it can be read at a distance.

Plan your visuals so that they, too, can be easily scanned and understood. Include captions.

Consider the most important thing you want people to understand as they look at your poster.

NOTE ON SCIENCE FAIR JUDGES: There's no guarantee the president will show up to talk to you at your booth, but you should prepare as if he or she will!

POSTER OR DISPLAY BOARD:
Scientists create these to help them show their work. Check the Internet for sample scientific posters and prize-winning science fair display boards. Your science poster gives a short-form version of your paper, write-up, or report, including:

- project title
- abstract
- question (the question the experiment was designed to answer)
- hypothesis
- background research
- materials
- procedure
- results
- conclusion
- future indications or questions

TALKING TO JUDGES AND OTHER VISITORS:

Plan what to say and how to say it. What's the most important point that you want to make when people ask you to tell them about your project? Know what information you want them to walk away with when they leave your booth.

Introduce yourself, giving your name loud and clear. Go on to give the name of your project and tell the subject of it. Tell what it was you wanted to find out and describe what you did to accomplish that. Then describe the data you gathered and explain what it told you about your topic. Finally, add a statement about what else you'd like to find out or what you want people to consider. Thank your listeners for their time, and take questions.

TALKING TIPS

Rehearse and time your statement and be ready to give it. Cut it if it's too long.

Ask someone to help you guess what kinds of questions you might be asked so that you can plan how to answer them.

SCIENCE STANDARDS

To align with Science, Technology, Engineering, Math (STEM), each experiment in this book has been correlated with the Next Generation Science Standards (NGSS), which are based on the Framework for K–12 Science Education developed by the National Research Council. Below you will find a list of each experiment in this book along with the standards they align to. At the end of each standard description you'll notice a number and some letters. These represent the grade level, subject area, and standard number for each standard (example: 4-LS1-1 represents a fourth grade standard, in life, physical, or earth and space science, standard number one). For more details on NGSS, visit nextgenscience.org. If you're more interested in the artistic merits of these activities, examine the grade-level National Coalition for Core Arts Standards (NCCAS) at nationalartsstandards.org.

COOL GLOW STICKS, Page 14
Standard(s)
Make observations and measurements to identify materials based on their properties. (5-PS1-3)

Develop a model that predicts and describes changes in particle motion, temperature, and state of a pure substance when thermal energy is added or removed. (MS-PS1-4)

FROZEN BUBBLES, Page 16
Standard(s)
Conduct an investigation to determine whether the mixing of two or more substances results in new substances. (5-PS1-4)

Develop a model that predicts and describes changes in particle motion, temperature, and state of a pure substance when thermal energy is added or removed. (MS-PS1-4)

DRIPPY STALACTITES, Page 19
Standard(s)
Plan and carry out fair tests in which variables are controlled and failure points are considered to identify aspects of a model or prototype that can be improved. (3–5-ETS1-3)

Develop a model to generate data for iterative testing and modification of a proposed object, tool, or process such that an optimal design can be achieved. (MS-ETS1-4)

GROW YOUR OWN SNOW, Page 22
Standard(s)
Conduct an investigation to determine whether the mixing of two or more substances results in new substances. (5-PS1-4)

Apply scientific principles to design, construct, and test a device that either minimizes or maximizes thermal energy transfer. (MS-PS3-3)

FREEZING IN TIME, Page 25
Standard(s)
Make observations and measurements to provide evidence of the effects of weathering or rate of erosion by water, ice, wind, or vegetation. (4-ESS2-1)

Develop a model to describe the cycling of Earth's materials and the flow of energy that drives this process. (MS-ESS2-1)

SUMMER SNOWBALL, Page 27
Standard(s)
Measure and graph quantities to provide evidence that regardless of the type of change that occurs when heating, cooling, or mixing substances, the total weight of matter is conserved. (5-PS1-2)

Develop a model that predicts and describes changes in particle motion, temperature, and state of a pure substance when thermal energy is added or removed. (MS-PS1-4)

SURVIVAL STILL, Page 32
Standard(s)
Develop a model to describe that matter is made of particles too small to be seen. (5-PS1-1)

Develop a model that predicts and describes changes in particle motion, temperature, and state of a pure substance when thermal energy is added or removed. (MS-PS1-4)

Pure, Sweet Water, Page 34
Standard(s)

Generate and compare multiple possible solutions to a problem based on how well each is likely to meet the criteria and constraint of the problem. (3–5-ETS1-2)

Evaluate competing design solutions using a systematic process to determine how well they meet the criteria and constraints of the problem. (MS-ETS1-2)

Ice Candle, Page 36
Standard(s)

Develop a model to describe that light reflecting from objects and entering the eye allows objects to be seen. (4-PS4-2)

Develop and use a model to describe that waves are reflected, absorbed, or transmitted through various materials. (MS-PS4-2)

Fire-Starter Ice, Page 38
Standard(s)

Apply scientific ideas to design, test, and refine a device that converts energy from one form to another. (4-PS3-4)

Develop and use a model to describe that waves are reflected, absorbed, or transmitted through various materials. (MS-PS4-2)

Orange Oil Lamp, Page 41
Standard(s)

Construct an argument that plants and animals have internal and external structures that function to

support survival, growth, behavior, and reproduction. (4-LS1-1)

Apply scientific principles to design, construct, and test a device that either minimizes or maximizes thermal energy transfer. (MS-PS3-3)

MYO Digital Microscope, Page 43
Standard(s)

Develop a model to describe that light reflecting from objects and entering the eye allows objects to be seen. (4-PS4-2)

Develop and use a model to describe that waves are reflected, absorbed, or transmitted through various materials. (MS-PS4-2)

That Sinking Feeling, Page 48
Standard(s)

Plan and conduct an investigation to provide evidence of the effects of balanced and unbalanced forces on the motion of an object. (3-PS2-1)

Plan an investigation to provide evidence that the change in an object's motion depends on the sum of the forces on the object and the mass of the object. (MS-PS2-2)

Miniature Marshmallow Gets Smaller, Page 50
Standard(s)

Develop a model to describe that matter is made of particles too small to be seen. (5-PS1-1)

Plan an investigation to provide evidence that the change in an object's motion depends on the sum of the forces on the object and the mass of the object. (MS-PS2-2)

Merry-Go-Round Catch, Page 52
Standard(s)

Plan and conduct an investigation to provide evidence of the effects of balanced and unbalanced forces on the motion of an object. (3-PS2-1)

Plan an investigation to provide evidence that the change in an object's motion depends on the sum of the forces on the object and the mass of the object. (MS-PS2-2)

Air Monster, Page 55
Standard(s)

Make observations to provide evidence that energy can be transferred from place to place by sound, light, heat, and electric currents. (4-PS3-2)

Develop a model that predicts and describes changes in particle motion, temperature, and state of a pure substance when thermal energy is added or removed. (MS-PS1-4)

Magic Arms, Page 58
Standard(s)

Plan and conduct an investigation to provide evidence of the effects of balanced and unbalanced forces on the motion of an object. (3-PS2-1)

Apply Newton's Third Law to design a solution to a problem involving the motion of two colliding objects. (MS-PS2-1)

Reindeer Vision, Page 62
Standard(s)

Construct an argument that plants and animals have internal and external structures that function to support survival, growth, behavior, and reproduction. (4-LS1-1)

Construct a scientific explanation based on evidence for how environmental and genetic factors influence the growth of organisms. (MS-LS1-5)

USE YOUR DOG'S HAIR AS WOOL, Page 64
Standard(s)

Make observations and/or measurements of an object's motion to provide evidence that a pattern can be used to predict future motion. (3-PS2-2)

Plan an investigation to provide evidence that the change in an object's motion depends on the sum of the forces on the object and the mass of the object. (MS-PS2-2)

SPIN WOOL INTO YARN, Page 66
Standard(s)

Plan and conduct an investigation to provide evidence of the effects of balanced and unbalanced forces on the motion of an object. (3-PS2-1)

Support an argument that the gravitational force exerted by Earth on objects is directed down. (5-PS2-1)

Plan an investigation to provide evidence that the change in an object's motion depends on the sum of the forces on the object and the mass of the object. (MS-PS2-2)

FINGER KNITTING, Page 68
Standard(s)

Plan and conduct an investigation to provide evidence of the effects of balanced and unbalanced forces on the motion of an object. (3-PS2-1)

Plan an investigation to provide evidence that the change in an object's motion depends on the sum of the forces on the object and the mass of the object. (MS-PS2-2)

INFRARED INTERFERENCE, Page 71
Standard(s)

Develop a model of waves to describe patterns in terms of amplitude and wavelength and that waves can cause objects to move. (4-PS4-1)

Develop and use a model to describe that waves are reflected, absorbed, or transmitted through various materials. (MS-PS4-2)

BLUBBER GLOVES, Page 74
Standard(s)

Construct an argument with evidence that in a particular habitat some organisms can survive well, some survive less well, and some cannot survive at all. (3-LS4-3)

Apply scientific principles to design, construct, and test a device that either minimizes or maximizes thermal energy transfer. (MS-PS3-3)

PAPER ENGINEERING, Page 78
Standard(s)

Plan and carry out fair tests in which variables are controlled and failure points are considered to identify aspects of a model or prototype that can be improved. (3-5-ETS1-3)

Develop a model to generate data for iterative testing and modification of a proposed object, tool, or process such that an optimal design can be achieved. (MS-ETS1-4)

ELEPHANT TOOTHPASTE, Page 80
Standard(s)

Conduct an investigation to determine whether the mixing of two or more substances results in new substances. (5-PS1-4)

Analyze and interpret data on the properties of substances before and after the substances interact to determine if a chemical reaction has occurred. (MS-PS1-2)

COLOR EXPLOSION, Page 82
Standard(s)

Develop a model to describe that matter is made of particles too small to be seen. (5-PS1-1)

Plan an investigation to provide evidence that the change in an object's motion depends on the sum of the forces on the object and the mass of the object. (MS-PS2-2)

DRY ICE BUBBLE, Page 84
Standard(s)

Conduct an investigation to determine whether the mixing of two or more substances results in new substances. (5-PS1-4)

Develop a model that predicts and describes changes in particle motion, temperature, and state of a pure substance when thermal energy is added or removed. (MS-PS1-4)

INSTANT SLUSH, Page 86
Standard(s)

Measure and graph quantities to provide evidence that regardless of the type of change that occurs when heating, cooling, or mixing substances, the total weight of matter is conserved. (5-PS1-2.)

Develop a model that predicts and describes changes in particle motion, temperature, and state of a pure substance when thermal energy is added or removed. (MS-PS1-4)

HUMAN SPIROGRAPH, Page 88
Standard(s)

Plan and conduct an investigation to provide evidence of the effects of balanced and unbalanced forces on the motion of an object. (3-PS2-1)

Plan an investigation to provide evidence that the change in an object's motion depends on the sum of the forces on the object and the mass of the object. (MS-PS2-2)

WIDE-ANGLE THEORY OF RELATIVITY, Page 90
Standard(s)

Use a model to describe that animals receive different types of information through their senses, process the information in their brain, and respond to the information in different ways. (4-LS1-2)

Gather and synthesize information that sensory receptors respond to stimuli by sending messages to the brain for immediate behavior or storage as memories. (MS-LS1-8)

A WEIRD PERSPECTIVE, Page 92
Standard(s)

Use a model to describe that animals receive different types of information through their senses, process the information in their brain, and respond to the information in different ways. (4-LS1-2)

Gather and synthesize information that sensory receptors respond to stimuli by sending messages to the brain for immediate behavior or storage as memories. (MS-LS1-8)

BATTERY COIL TRAIN, Page 94
Standard(s)

Define a simple design problem that can be solved by applying scientific ideas about magnets. (3-PS2-4)

Conduct an investigation and evaluate the experimental design to provide evidence that fields exist between objects exerting forces on each other even though the objects are not in contact. (MS-PS2-5)

BOTTLE OF STRING, Page 96
Standard(s)

Plan and carry out fair tests in which variables are controlled and failure points are considered to identify aspects of a model or prototype that can be improved. (3-5-ETS1-3)

Develop a model to generate data for iterative testing and modification of a proposed object, tool, or process such that an optimal design can be achieved. (MS-ETS1-4)

MYO LASER POINTER, Page 100
Standard(s)

Make observations to provide evidence that energy can be transferred from place to place by sound, light, heat, and electric currents. (4-PS3-2)

Develop and use a model to describe that waves are reflected, absorbed, or transmitted through various materials. (MS-PS4-2)

HYDROPHOBIC GLASS GRAPHICS, Page 102
Standard(s)

Make observations and measurements to identify materials based on their properties. (5-PS1-4)

Plan an investigation to provide evidence that the change in an object's motion depends on the sum of the forces on the object and the mass of the object. (MS-PS2-2)

HYDROPHOBIC CLOTHES, Page 104
Standard(s)

Plan and carry out fair tests in which variables are controlled and failure points are considered to identify aspects of a model or prototype that can be improved. (3–5-ETS1-3)

Analyze data from tests to determine similarities and differences among several design solutions to identify the best characteristics of each that can be combined into a new solution to better meet the criteria for success. (MS-ETS1-3)

RAINY DAY SURPRISE, Page 107
Standard(s)

Make observations and measurements to identify materials based on their properties. (5-PS1-4)

Plan an investigation to provide evidence that the change in an object's motion depends on the sum of the forces on the object and the mass of the object. (MS-PS2-2)

HERO'S ENGINE, Page 109
Standard(s)

Plan and conduct an investigation to provide evidence of the effects of balanced and unbalanced forces on the motion of an object. (3-PS2-1)

Apply scientific ideas to design, test, and refine a device that converts energy from one form to another. (4-PS3-4)

Construct, use, and present arguments to support the claim that when the kinetic energy of an object changes, energy is transferred to or from the object. (MS-PS3-5)

STEM

Scaredy Sand, Page 112
Standard(s)

Make observations and measurements to identify materials based on their properties. (5-PS1-4)

Plan an investigation to provide evidence that the change in an object's motion depends on the sum of the forces on the object and the mass of the object. (MS-PS2-2)

Bottle Won't Pour, Page 114
Standard(s)

Develop a model to describe that matter is made of particles too small to be seen. (5-PS1-1)

Plan an investigation to provide evidence that the change in an object's motion depends on the sum of the forces on the object and the mass of the object. (MS-PS2-2)

Peeps Zap, Page 118
Standard(s)

Develop a model of waves to describe patterns in terms of amplitude and wavelength and that waves can cause objects to move. (4-PS4-1)

Use mathematical representations to describe a simple model for waves that includes how the amplitude of a wave is related to the energy in a wave. (MS-PS4-1)

Backyard Bioblitz, Page 121
Standard(s)

Develop a model to describe the movement of matter among plants, animals, decomposers, and the environment. (5-LS2-1)

Analyze and interpret data to provide evidence for the effects of resource availability on organisms and populations of organisms in an ecosystem. (MS-LS2-1)

Liquid Lens, Page 125
Standard(s)

Develop a model to describe the movement of matter among plants, animals, decomposers, and the environment. (5-LS2-1)

Construct an explanation that predicts patterns of interactions among organisms across multiple ecosystems. (MS-LS2-2)

Bacteriart, Page 128
Standard(s)

Develop models to describe that organisms have unique and diverse life cycles but all have in common birth, growth, reproduction, and death. (3-LS1-1)

Construct a scientific explanation based on evidence for how environmental and genetic factors influence the growth of organisms. (MS-LS1-5)

Myo Incubator, Page 131
Standard(s)

Apply scientific ideas to design, test, and refine a device that converts energy from one form to another. (4-PS3-4)

Apply scientific principles to design, construct, and test a device that either minimizes or maximizes thermal energy transfer. (MS-PS3-3)

Eco-Cooler, Page 133
Standard(s)

Plan and conduct an investigation to provide evidence of the effects of balanced and unbalanced forces on the motion of an object. (3-PS2-1)

Plan an investigation to provide evidence that the change in an object's motion depends on the sum of the forces on the object and the mass of the object. (MS-PS2-2)

Myo OOHO, Page 136
Standard(s)

Obtain and combine information about ways individual communities use science ideas to protect the Earth's resources and environment. (5-ESS3-1)

Apply scientific principles to design a method for monitoring and minimizing a human impact on the environment. (MS-ESS3-3)

THE INDEX

Instructions for experiments are indicated by **boldface.**

INDEX

ACKNOWLEDGMENTS

Thank you to:

Christina Ascani

Gwen Balogh

Faye Bender

Courtney Caplan, dog groomer

Doug Dickinson and the Sheep
Shoppe, Newtown, Connecticut

Clancy Emanuel and the ROV
Shop aboard E/V *Nautilus*

Lori Epstein

Jeff Heimsath

Grace Hill

Amy Kefauver

Amanda Larsen

Priyanka Lamichhane

Shira Evans

Dr. Kenneth G. Libbrecht

Sarah Mock

Angela Modany

Julye Newlin

Ocean Exploration Trust, the DSV
Hercules/Argus team, and the
crew of E/V *Nautilus*

DJ Pevey

Jon and Terry Poirier, Tailwaggers,
Bethel, Connecticut

Sanjida Rashid

Tucker Smith

Hilda Valdespino

Tirzah Weiskotten

Dr. Norbert E. Yankielun

Mark Young

Sam Young

and most of all,
Matthew Rakola

CREDITS

Since 1888, the National Geographic Society has funded
more than 12,000 research, exploration, and preservation
projects around the world. The Society receives funds from
National Geographic Partners, LLC, funded in part by your
purchase. A portion of the proceeds from this book sup-
ports this vital work. To learn more, visit natgeo.com/info.

Photo Credits:
All photos are by Matthew Rakola unless noted below.
Cover (boy scientist), Mark Thiessen, NG Staff; 6, Michael J
Thompson/Shutterstock; 7, Mega Pixel/Shutterstock; 8,
Mark Thiessen, NG Staff; 51, Photo by Julye Newlin/cour-
tesy of the author; 148, Win McNamee/Getty Images; 149
(both), Gabbro/Alamy Stock Photo; 159, Christina Ascani/
NG Staff

For more information, visit nationalgeographic.com, call
1-800-647-5463, or write to the following address:

National Geographic Partners
1145 17th Street N.W.
Washington, D.C. 20036-4688 U.S.A.

Visit us online at nationalgeographic.com/books

For librarians and teachers: ngchildrensbooks.org

More for kids from National Geographic:
kids.nationalgeographic.com

For information about special discounts for bulk
purchases, please contact National Geographic Books
Special Sales: specialsales@natgeo.com

For rights or permissions inquiries, please contact
National Geographic Books Subsidiary Rights:
bookrights@natgeo.com

Art directed and designed by Sanjida Rashid

Trade paperback edition ISBN: 978-1-4263-2863-3
Library edition ISBN: 978-1-4263-2864-0

Printed in Hong Kong
17/THK/1

CONVERSION TO METRIC MEASURES

WHEN YOU KNOW	MULTIPLY BY	TO FIND
LENGTH		
inches (in)	2.54	centimeters
feet (ft)	0.30	meters
yards (yd)	0.91	meters
miles (mi)	1.61	kilometers
MASS		
ounces (oz)	28.35	grams
pounds (lb)	0.45	kilograms
TEMPERATURE		
degrees Fahrenheit (°F)	5/9 after subtracting 32	degrees Celsius (centigrade)

CONVERSION FROM METRIC MEASURES

WHEN YOU KNOW	MULTIPLY BY	TO FIND
LENGTH		
centimeters (cm)	0.39	inches
meters (m)	3.28	feet
meters (m)	1.09	yards
kilometers (km)	0.62	miles
VOLUME		
liters (L)	2.11	pints
liters (L)	1.06	quarts
liters (L)	0.26	gallons